Jordan

Frontispiece: **Market**

Consultant: Sean L. Yom, Associate Professor of Political Science,
Temple University, Philadelphia, PA

Please note: All statistics are as up-to-date as possible at the time of publication.

Book production by The Design Lab

Library of Congress Cataloging-in-Publication Data
Names: Sonneborn, Liz, author.
Title: Jordan / by Liz Sonneborn.
Description: New York : Children's Press, an imprint of Scholastic Inc.,
    2019. | Series: Enchantment of the world | Includes bibliographical
    references and index.
Identifiers: LCCN 2018019518 | ISBN 9780531126981 (library binding : alk.
    paper)
Subjects: LCSH: Jordan—Juvenile literature.
Classification: LCC DS153 .S56 2019 | DDC 956.95—dc23
LC record available at https://lccn.loc.gov/2018019518

Scholastic Inc., 557 Broadway, New York, NY 10012

1 2 3 4 5 6 7 8 9 10 R 28 27 26 25 24 23 22 21 20 19

Jordan

BY LIZ SONNEBORN

Enchantment of the World™
Second Series

CHILDREN'S PRESS®

An Imprint of Scholastic Inc.

Contents

Left to right: **Coral reef, Bedouin woman, Arabian oryx, jewelry, Petra**

CHAPTER 1

A Reluctant King

I N JULY 1998, KING HUSSEIN, THE RULER OF THE SMALL Middle Eastern country of Jordan, made a live TV address. He told his people that he was being treated for cancer. The news set off a wave of panic in Jordan's capital, Amman. For many Jordanians, their country without King Hussein was almost unthinkable. He had been on the throne for nearly fifty years and was the only leader most Jordanians had ever known.

Amman was also abuzz with the question of who would take King Hussein's place after he died. The answer seemed to be Hassan, Hussein's brother. Hassan was the crown prince, which placed him next in line for the kingship. But some elites were not sure about Hassan. They were angling to elevate Hamzah, Hussein's eighteen-year-old son, to crown prince so he could become the new king. Hamzah was the oldest son Hussein had had with his current wife, Queen Noor.

Opposite: **Roughly two thousand years ago at Petra, the site of an ancient city in southern Jordan, large structures were carved into stone. Al-Khaznah, "the Treasury," was the tomb of a king.**

Rumors Spread

While the royal court gossiped and plotted, King Hussein was in the United States receiving treatment for his disease. But even that far away, he got wind of the rumors swirling around Amman.

The king wanted to know exactly what was going on. He asked his visiting son, Abdullah, his eldest child with his second wife, to fill him in. King Hussein especially wanted to know if it was true that Prince Hassan had started hiring and firing military officers, taking over the king's role as commander in chief without his permission. Abdullah confirmed that this was true. But he also assured his father that the military, still loyal to the king, was ignoring Hassan's orders. Angry with Hassan, the king told Abdullah that he was thinking of changing the line of succession.

A Final Trip Home

In the months that followed, the international press began to make wild speculations about Jordan. Their headlines told tales of palace intrigue. "Princes Jostle for Hussein's Crown," one declared.

Abdullah tried to ignore the hubbub, instead concentrating on helping his father. By early January 1999, that meant preparing for King Hussein's trip home so that he could see Jordan one last time.

Piloting his own plane, King Hussein arrived at the airport. He stepped out onto the runway, wearing a dark business suit and a kaffiyeh, a traditional Jordanian red-and-white headscarf. Although the king walked forward with resolve, he looked frailer than ever.

Greeting Friends and Enemies

King Hussein made his way down a welcoming line full of Jordanian politicians and members of the royal court. Abdullah later recalled the king's behavior as "a quiet lesson in statecraft." With each greeting, Hussein sent a not-so-subtle signal about how he felt about each person, based on how they had acted in the six months he was away.

He kissed or hugged those most in his favor. He shook the hand of those he still respected. But when he came upon people he felt had been disloyal to him, he merely walked right past them, ignoring their very presence. When one family member tried to kiss him, King Hussein pushed him out of the way.

When King Hussein reached Abdullah, he held out his palm. But while they shook hands, his father looked off in the distance. The king then quickly moved along to the next person in the line.

In an instant, Abdullah knew what his father's chilly greeting meant. The king was not unhappy with Abdullah. On the contrary, he was going to make Abdullah crown prince. But the king did not want to tip his hand until he had made a formal announcement, for fear others in the court would begin conspiring against Abdullah.

A Relatively Normal Life

When Abdullah was born in 1962, as Hussein's first son, he automatically became crown prince. But when he was three, the king decided his brother Hassan, who had just turned eighteen, should take on that role.

The decision was practical. Abdullah I, the first king of Jordan and Hussein's grandfather, had been shot and killed by an assassin. Hussein himself had already survived several assassination attempts. He did not expect to live much longer so he thought it best that an adult be in line to succeed him. Abdullah later said removing him as crown prince "was one

of the best things [my father] ever did for me, as it allowed me to lead a relatively normal life."

Concerned for Abdullah's safety, his parents sent him off to boarding school first in England and then the United States. He then prepared for a career in the military, attending the Royal Military Academy Sandhurst in the United Kingdom.

King Hussein with his son Prince Abdullah in 1993. The family is said to be directly descended from Muhammad, the prophet of Islam.

Taking Charge

King Hussein died on February 7, 1999. The next day, his son was sworn in as Abdullah II, the fourth king of Jordan. As he took the throne, Abdullah II realized that his father had prepared him for the kingship in ways other than sending him to military school. Hussein had also taken him on trips

throughout Jordan and on state visits to other countries, so he could see what a king did. "I was with my father [during many] crises," he later explained. "But I didn't have the spotlight on me. I was watching and learning without having the pressures on me."

Abdullah, too, had spent most of his life outside of politics, which he now saw as an advantage. He rejected much of the pomp and ceremony of his position. King Abdullah also did not talk like other politicians, getting lost in flowery phrases or confusing jargon. His blunt, direct way of speaking appealed to many Jordanians.

An honor guard accompanies the coffin carrying the body of King Hussein. About eight hundred thousand Jordanians turned out for the funeral procession.

An Uncertain Future

Abdullah's initial popularity gave him confidence. Soon after becoming king, he told a reporter, "Our country has a lot of challenges, but I think they are all manageable." However, as it soon became clear, Abdullah was overly optimistic. He had promised to give the people more of a say in their government and to work to make the economy stronger. But every reform he proposed was met with resistance. Many people in the royal family and other powerful people did not want to see things changed. They opposed his reforms, fearing that they would lose their special privileges.

When Abdullah failed to change the system, many other Jordanians became angry. They accused Abdullah of making false promises. They said that he was pretending to want democratic reform, when all he was really interested in was propping up the monarchy.

While trying to unite his people, Abdullah has also had to deal with foreign threats. Jordan's tense relationship with Israel, its neighbor to the west, has long been a source of anxiety. But during his reign, the king has also had to worry about wars that broke out in other nearby nations, such as Iraq and Syria. Not only did he have to struggle to keep Jordan out of these violent conflicts, but he also had to deal with floods of refugees and an increased risk of terrorist attacks.

Despite these challenges, like his father, Abdullah II has managed to keep Jordan fairly stable during his reign. But as he has admitted publicly, the pressure on him is so great he has often thought about stepping down from the throne. Although the reluctant king has so far resisted that temptation, he has already made plans for a Jordan without him in charge. In 2009, Abdullah formally named his then teenage son Hussein as the new crown prince. Like his father and grandfather before him, Hussein is well aware that ruling Jordan, as it heads into an uncertain future, will be a difficult and sometimes thankless job. As Abdullah explained, "When I made [Hussein] crown prince, I don't think he was very happy. . . . I don't think he was happy with me at all."

CHAPTER 2

Highlands and Deserts

JORDAN IS LOCATED IN THE NORTHWESTERN CORNER OF the Arabian Peninsula, a region of southwest Asia. Covering 34,495 square miles (89,342 square kilometers), Jordan is slightly smaller than the U.S. state of Indiana.

To the north of Jordan is the country of Syria. To the east is Iraq, and to the south and southeast is Saudi Arabia. Along its western border is the Jordan River, which gives Jordan its name. On the other side of the river are Israel and the West Bank. Jordan controlled the West Bank from 1948 to 1967. The West Bank is now disputed territory. It is claimed by both the Israelis and the Palestinians.

Three Regions

Jordan can be divided into three geographic regions. In the far west is the Jordan River valley. This narrow strip running from

Opposite: **Wind and water have carved the rock into dramatic shapes at Wadi Rum in southern Jordan.**

Jordan's Geographic Features

Area: 34,495 square miles (89,342 sq km)

Length of Coastline: 16 miles (26 km)

Longest Border: With Saudi Arabia, 454 miles (731 km)

Longest River: Jordan, about 200 miles (320 km)

Largest Lake: Dead Sea, 234 square miles (606 sq km)

Highest Elevation: 6,083 feet (1,854 m), at Umm ad Dami

Lowest Elevation: 1,414 feet (431 m) below sea level, at the Dead Sea

Average High Temperature: In Amman, 55°F (13°C) in January, 90°F (32°C) in July

Average Low Temperature: In Amman, 40°F (4°C) in January, 69°F (21°C) in July

Largest City: Amman, population 1,275,857

Average Annual Precipitation: 11 inches (28 cm) in Amman

north to south has some of Jordan's best farmland. An area in the northern valley called the Ghor is particularly fertile.

Crops flourish in the Jordan River valley.

Directly to the east of the Jordan River valley are the highlands. This hilly area runs like a spine down the length of western Jordan. The highlands rise to an average of about 3,000 feet (900 meters) above sea level. Hills in the south are even taller. There lies Umm ad Dami. With a peak that reaches an elevation of 6,083 feet (1,854 m), it is the highest point in all of Jordan.

The northern portion of the highlands is home to the majority of Jordan's population. It includes the cities of Irbid and Zarqa as well as Amman, the nation's capital. The weather in the highlands is generally comfortable. During the long summer, temperatures top out at about 90 degrees Fahrenheit (32 degrees Celsius). In the short winter, temperatures can

The Khamsin

Every spring, the residents of Amman steel themselves for the khamsin. These hot, dry winds blow southeast from the deserts of the Arabian Peninsula. With them come dust and sand that darken the sky and cover everything with a coat of grit. The word *khamsin* means "fifty" in Arabic. Traditionally, the khamsin were said to blow for fifty days. In Amman, the dusty winds only last a few days, although, with the discomfort they bring, it feels like much longer.

drop to about 50°F (10°C). The winter is also the rainy season. Amman sees about 11 inches (28 centimeters) of rain each year.

The highlands gradually slope downward toward desert lands in the east. This geographical region is by far the largest in Jordan. The eastern deserts make up about 90 percent of the country, but hold only about 5 percent of Jordan's population. Most of the hot and dry desert lands are virtually uninhabitable.

During the day, the temperature often rises well above 100°F (38°C), although it can drop to freezing at night. The area receives only a scant 2 inches (5 cm) of rain each year. The eastern deserts are so forbidding that their only residents are the Bedouins. These people survive by traveling from place to place in search of the deserts' meager water sources.

Rivers, Lakes, and Wadis

The most important water source in Jordan is the Jordan River. Stretching roughly 200 miles (320 km), it is the longest river in the country. Its major tributaries are the Zarqa and the Yarmouk. The Yarmouk forms part of Jordan's border with Syria. The Jordan River is fed by the Sea of Galilee, also called Lake Tiberias, which lies to the north in Israel. Its waters empty into the Dead Sea to the south.

Despite its name, the Dead Sea is actually a lake. With an area of 234 square miles (606 sq km), it is Jordan's largest.

For much of its course, the Jordan River runs along the border between Jordan and Israel.

Urban Landscapes

Located in northwest Jordan, the capital of Amman is the country's largest city by far. Jordan's next biggest urban centers are nearby. The cities of Zarqa, Irbid, and Russeifa are all within an hour's drive of the capital.

Just 12 miles (19 km) northeast of Amman lies Zarqa, which is home to about 800,000 people. Once primarily known for its military bases, it is now a major industrial city. Over several decades, Zarqa took in large numbers of Palestinian refugees. Today, more than half of its residents are of Palestinian heritage.

Irbid has been inhabited for thousands of years. Today, with a population of about 300,000, it is best known as the location of Yarmouk University, one of the Middle East's greatest institutions of higher learning. In this

Cars fill the roads in busy Irbid.

lively college town, students gather day and night at Irbid's many restaurants and music stores. The city also has a wide variety of cultural institutions, including the Jordan Natural History Museum and the Museum of Jordanian Heritage. Irbid's population has grown quickly in recent years as refugees have crossed the Syrian border to settle in and around the city.

Russeifa is the fourth-largest city in Jordan, with about 270,000 residents. Located on the Zarqa River, it is also an important industrial center. One of its biggest employers is the Jordan Phosphate Mines. Long suffering from a lack of water, Russeifa, with funding from the Chinese government, is now working to improve its water supply.

Buildings blanket the hills in Zarqa.

However, Jordan's border with Israel runs down the center of the lake, so Jordan controls only the Dead Sea's eastern half.

A woman floats in the Dead Sea.

The bottom of the Dead Sea is the lowest place on earth. It lies at 1,414 feet (431 m) below sea level. The Dead Sea is notable for the saltiness of its water. It is about ten times as salty as the Atlantic Ocean. The mineral content of the Dead Sea is so high that no marine life larger than bacteria can survive in it. Unlucky fish are sometimes swept into the Dead Sea from the Jordan River, only to die when they come in contact with its salty water.

For thousands of years, people have come to wade in the Dead Sea. Its waters have long been thought to have healing

Plants grow around the site of Lawrence's Spring.

While living in the Middle East, T. E. Lawrence adopted the clothing styles of the local people.

Lawrence's Spring

In Wadi Rum in southern Jordan, a natural spring rises up from the brick-red sand. For thousands of years, it served as a watering hole for caravans traveling through this forbidding landscape.

The pool of water is now known as Lawrence's Spring. It is named after T. E. Lawrence, a British archaeologist, author, and adventurer. Lawrence embraced the culture and clothing of the Bedouin people who lived near Wadi Rum. In 1916, during the Arab Revolt, he joined the Bedouin in their rebellion against the Ottoman Empire.

Lawrence's story inspired the classic movie *Lawrence of Arabia* (1962). Filmed partly in Wadi Rum, it helped spark Jordan's tourist industry. After seeing the movie, fans wanted to travel to Jordan and see the magnificent landscapes featured in the film. Lawrence's Spring is now a leading attraction for travelers who want to follow in the footsteps of Lawrence of Arabia.

powers. The water is so dense with minerals that people float easily, without any effort. The salty water stings terribly when it gets in people's eyes and noses.

Much of Jordan has no water source. But in some areas, wadis, or dry valleys, can temporarily fill with rainwater. The largest wadi is Wadi Rum. Located in southern Jordan, Wadi Rum is known for its spectacular sandstone cliffs and bright red-colored dunes. Because of its otherworldly look, several movies have been filmed at Wadi Rum. For example, in *The Martian* (2015), its landscapes stood in for the surface of the planet Mars.

Jordan is completely landlocked except at its southernmost tip. There, its short 16-mile (26 km) coastline borders the Gulf of Aqaba, an arm of the Red Sea. The city of Aqaba is

Aqaba is a popular resort.

Jordan's only port. It is also a tourist center. Visitors come to enjoy its beaches and to swim and snorkel in the gulf waters.

Water Woes

A mostly desert nation, Jordan has never had a lot of drinkable water. In the past, this did not present much of a problem. Jordan's population was so small that its limited water supply was large enough.

In recent decades, though, Jordan's lack of water has become a growing problem. The many refugees arriving from neighboring countries have increased the demand for water. At the same time, Jordan's water supply is dwindling. The global climate change caused by an increase of pollutants in the atmosphere is affecting Jordan severely. As the climate changes, the country's rainfall is expected to drop about 30 percent by the year 2100. Jordan is on track to become the first nation in the world to completely run out of water.

The government is taking action to prevent this disaster. Schools teach students about water conservation. Authorities are cracking down on water thieves, who reroute water pipes and sell the water they steal at high prices. And farmers are being urged to modernize their agricultural practices to use less water.

Jordan is also teaming up with Israel on a project to produce more drinkable water. The two countries plan to build a plant in the city of Aqaba to take salt out of water from the Red Sea. The desalinated water would then be piped to communities in both countries. Long-standing tensions between Jordan and Israel have stalled the project. Building the plant

The land around the Dead Sea is crumbling, as deep and dangerous sinkholes appear.

Saving the Dead Sea

The region around the Dead Sea is facing an ecological disaster. The reason is that the sea's water level is dropping fast. In the past, the Jordan River flowed freely into the Dead Sea, replenishing its waters. But now both Jordan and Israel divert river water to use on farms and in homes. As a result, the water level in the Dead Sea is sinking about 3 feet (1 m) each year.

As the water drops, fresh water has been seeping into the salty land along the Dead Sea's shores. This water dissolves the salt, causing the land just under the surface to be eaten away.

With nothing to hold it up, the surface can suddenly collapse into deep sinkholes. There are more than one thousand sinkholes around the Dead Sea. They have swallowed up trees, roads, buildings, and even people. If water levels continue to recede, the Dead Sea and the land around it will soon be destroyed.

One plan to save the Dead Sea involves a canal known as the Red-Dead. This canal would allow water from the Red Sea to flow into the Dead Sea. It would also bring a new water supply to northern Jordan.

will also be expensive. The current estimated cost stands at $10 billion, but it could easily rise higher. Facing a society without water, Jordanians have to do whatever is possible to collect every drop of water they can.

CHAPTER 3

Wild Jordan

MOST OF JORDAN IS DESERT, AN ENVIRONMENT where few creatures can survive. Nevertheless, the country is home to a wide array of plants and animals. The western portion of Jordan has a variety of habitats where many living things thrive. But even its deserts are rich in species that are well adapted to its dry, hot climate.

Opposite: **Hardy flowers grow in the dry land of Jordan.**

Plant Life

There are about two thousand different types of plants in Jordan. Most are found in the Jordan River valley or the western highlands. In the highlands, winter rains feed flowers that produce brilliant blooms throughout the spring. Native wildflowers include poppies, daisies, crocuses, orchids, and hollyhocks. The many varieties of flowers that thrive in Jordan are showcased at the newly opened Royal Botanic Garden.

The Black Iris

In the spring, wildflowers sprout up throughout western Jordan. But one bloom is a particularly welcome sight—the rare black iris, Jordan's national flower.

Contrary to its name, the black iris is colored a deep, dark purple. Three of its glossy petals grow upright, while three more droop downward. The flower looks delicate, but it is a hardy species that can survive under harsh sunlight in dry soil.

The black iris does not grow well in gardens. It only thrives in the wild. As farms have encroached on its natural habitat, the plant has become endangered. It is also threatened by goats, which like to chomp on its beautiful flowers.

In Jordan, the black iris is considered a symbol of growth and renewal.

Forests cover only about 1 percent of Jordan's land. Most of the country's trees are found in the highlands, although some palms grow near desert springs. Highland trees include oaks, pines, pistachios, and cinnabars. Small strawberry trees are also common. Farmers grow orchards of fig trees and olives trees.

Vegetation in Jordan's deserts includes bushes, shrubs, and grasses. They often grow along the sides and floors of valleys that collect the little rainwater that falls in the region. These drought-resistant plants are vital to the way of life of the Bedouin people. The plants provide food for the herds of goats and sheep the Bedouin raise.

Mammals

The most abundant mammals in Jordan are small creatures, such as mice, rats, and rabbits. Jordan's forests are home to

Palm trees grow along cliffs in Jordan.

The camels in Jordan are dromedaries, which have one hump.

How to Ride a Camel

For thousands of years, the Bedouin people of Jordan navigated through the desert on the backs of camels. The riders wrapped their left leg around the animals' solitary hump. They then hooked their left foot under the right knee, leaving their right foot to hang down. Secured in this way, the Bedouin people were sure to stay on top of their camels, even as they raced across the sand.

Today, Bedouin are more likely to travel in four-wheel-drive trucks or in dune buggies than atop a camel. Most Bedouin who still keep a camel herd are employed in the tourist industry. They serve as guides for adventurous travelers who want to explore Wadi Rum or other desert sites on camelback just as the Bedouin once did.

Other Bedouin people ride camels as part of their work for the Royal Desert Forces. These police officers scour the eastern deserts, looking for smugglers or hunters shooting illegal prey. While most of the force rides in vehicles, some patrol on camels. By following this Bedouin tradition, the Royal Desert Forces can more easily earn the trust and respect of the people they serve.

porcupines and Persian squirrels. Jerboas are frequently seen in the desert. These rodents look like tiny kangaroos. Their strong hind legs allow them to hop through sand at high speeds. In rocky areas, rock hyraxes can be seen scurrying about. The rock hyrax looks like a large guinea pig but is in fact a close relative of the elephant.

Larger mammals native to Jordan include jackals, foxes, wolves, hyenas, and boars. Some of the nation's most spectacular animals, however, are facing extinction. Well adapted to the deserts around Wadi Araba in southern Jordan, the dorcas gazelle is becoming rare in the wild. This small sand-colored

Rock hyraxes come out of their shelters only for short periods each day to feed. They eat grass, fruits, and leaves.

Both male and female Arabian oryx have long horns.

The Arabian Oryx

The eastern deserts of Jordan were long the home of the majestic Arabian oryx. Now Jordan's national animal, the oryx is a type of antelope. An adult oryx stands about 40 inches (100 cm) high, from hoof to shoulder, and weighs between 120 and 150 pounds (55 and 70 kilograms).

The Arabian oryx is perfectly suited to a desert habitat. Most of its fur is white so it deflects sunlight. Its brown legs, however, hold in heat, keeping the animal warm on cold desert mornings. The oryx also has wide hoofs that allow it to walk smoothly over sand.

The oryx's ability to smell rain from miles away also helps it survive in the harsh desert. It can live on small amounts of water for days or even weeks at a time. Just the dew on the grasses it eats is enough to satisfy the oryx's thirst.

The Arabian oryx has even survived what once seemed like certain extinction. By the early 1970s, hunters killed the last few remaining oryx in the wild. Breeding programs of conservation groups and zoos, however, brought the oryx back from the brink. There are now seven thousand oryx in captivity. Another one thousand live in protected wildlife areas.

gazelle can run as fast as 50 miles (80 km) an hour to escape predators. Nubian ibexes now survive only within protected areas in Jordan. The most notable trait of these rugged creatures is their horns, particularly those of males. Their enormous, ridged horns curve backward, almost creating a complete circle.

The animal most prized by Jordan's royal family is the Arabian horse. Known by their high ears and arched tails, the breed has long played an important role in Bedouin culture. Established by King Abdullah I, the Royal Stables outside of Amman house 250 Arabian horses. The bloodlines of some of these treasured animals can be traced back for hundreds of years.

Other Creatures

Just about everywhere in Jordan, there are many reptiles and insects. Scorpions, spiders, moths, grasshoppers, dragonflies, and beetles are found in its various habitats. About three dozen types of snakes are native to the country. Most are harmless, but five venomous species—including the Palestine viper—have a dangerous bite.

The desert is home to many species of lizards, including the large desert monitor. It can grow to be 50 inches (130 cm) long. The male Sinai agama is one of Jordan's most beautiful lizards. During breeding season, the male turns a bright blue color.

About twenty species of freshwater fish swim in Jordan's rivers and streams. But most of the country's fish and marine life are found off its short coastline. Nearly one thousand types of fish live in the Gulf of Aqaba, including groupers,

Coral reefs have many crevices where small fish can hide from predators.

parrotfish, and boxfish, which true to their name have a square shape. Other marine life in the gulf includes crabs, shrimp, eels, and seahorses. Many of these creatures find shelter in the large coral reefs in the gulf's waters.

Throughout the year, birds flock to Jordan. Some are year-round residents, including a few species found only in the Middle East. Among them are the Arabian warbler, the sooty falcon, the sand partridge, and Hume's tawny owl. Jordan's national bird is the Sinai rosefinch. Its pink-hued feathers are the same color as the stone ruins of the ancient city of Petra. Another colorful native bird is the Palestine sunbird, whose plumage is a brilliant blue.

Other birds visit Jordan during their yearly migrations. Many, including herons, pelicans, and egrets, stop at the desert oasis of Azraq. The Azraq Wetland Reserve is a favorite spot for bird-watchers. The area attracts more than two hundred species of migrating birds from Asia, Africa, and Europe.

Protecting Nature

During the late twentieth century, the plant and animal life of Jordan faced many threats. As forests were cut down and rivers were dammed, many living things lost their natural habitats. Air and water pollution also endangered the places they lived. For large animals, hunters posed the greatest hazard. Shooting automatic weapons from high-speed vehicles, hunters killed

Hoopoes, which can be found at Azraq, are famed for their crown of feathers.

A visitor admires the landscape at Dana Nature Reserve.

so many animals that some species, such as the Arabian oryx and the Asiatic lion, became extinct in the wild in Jordan.

Jordan is now working to preserve its natural habitats and the plants and animals that live in them. Central to this mission is the Royal Society for the Conservation of Nature. The first organization of its kind in the Middle East, it is working to restore Jordan's lost forestlands and form environmental clubs for young people.

The Royal Society also supports many reserves that protect some of Jordan's most vulnerable natural treasures. Among them is the Dana Nature Reserve, which preserves an area of rocky cliffs and sand dunes where some two hundred species of animals and six hundred species of plants live. The Shaumari Wildlife Reserve runs a breeding program to save endangered species. And the Aqaba Marine Park protects the coral reefs and beaches that line Jordan's southern coast.

A Second Chance for Abused Animals

Princess Alia of Jordan, a daughter of King Hussein, is on a mission. She wants to provide abused animals throughout the Middle East with a safe home. With this goal in mind, she partnered with the organization Four Paws to open the Al Ma'wa Wildlife Reserve near Amman in 2016.

Since then, this refuge has taken in a variety of animals, from stray dogs to former circus-performing bears. Many are lions and tigers that were bred on farms in Jordan, Iraq, and Syria. The animals were then smuggled into oil-rich neighboring countries, where they were sold to wealthy people as pets. In these illegal zoos, the animals were actively mistreated or not cared for properly. The Al Ma'wa Wildlife Reserve tries to rehabilitate these abused animals and, if they are native to Jordan, eventually release them into the wild. Funded

Princess Alia greets a young lion.

by the United Arab Emirates, the growing sanctuary aims to become the biggest wildlife preserve in the Middle East.

In 2017, a lion rescued from a zoo in Syria gave birth to a cub at Al Ma'wa Wildlife Reserve.

CHAPTER 4

Young Nation, Ancient Land

T HE COUNTRY OF JORDAN CAME INTO EXISTENCE IN 1946, but its lands have been home to many different peoples since ancient times. Throughout its early history, a series of foreigners entered and occupied what is now Jordan. They were attracted by both its fertile lands in the northwest and its lucrative trade routes. Each group built its own civilization there before being overtaken by another group determined to claim the valuable land for themselves.

Opposite: **The remains of a Roman city stand at Jarash in northwestern Jordan.**

Early Kingdoms

Human beings may have been living in the region that is now Jordan as early as 17,000 BCE. These people survived by hunting game and gathering wild plants. By about 8500 BCE, humans there began living in more permanent villages. They started to grow crops and raise animal herds for their meat and milk.

The Ain Ghazal Statues

In 1974, while a crew was building a road near Amman, a bulldozer unearthed something amazing—a collection of statues that had been buried for some nine thousand years.

The Ain Ghazal statues are among the oldest statues depicting human beings ever found. Some of them depict full bodies, although they are smaller than life-size, measuring about 3 feet (1 m) tall. Others are busts, which depict just the head and shoulders.

The statues were created with frames made from reeds and grasses. The frames were then coated with plaster. The bodies have few details. Ancient artisans, however, spent a good deal of care crafting the faces. Molded plaster creates their mouths, noses, and brows. But their eyes are their most arresting feature. They are filled with white chalk and outlined with black bitumen, an asphalt-like substance. Bitumen was also used to draw a vertical pupil at the center of each eye.

The large eyes give the sculptures a haunting quality. But one sculpture is particularly eerie. It depicts a single body with two heads.

Thirty ancient human sculptures were discovered at Ain Ghazal, near Amman.

After 1200 BCE, three kingdoms grew up in the region of Jordan—Ammon, Moab, and Edom. About three hundred years later, they were attacked by armies of Israelites led by

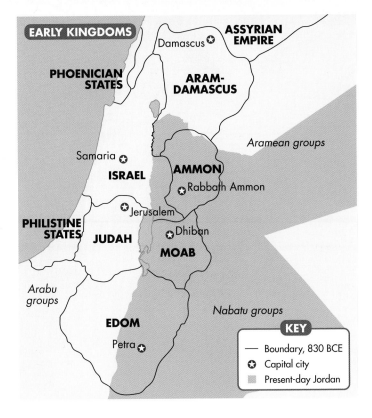

King David, whose story appears in the Bible. After his death, however, the Israelites lost Jordan when Mesha, the king of Moab, staged a successful rebellion.

In the following centuries, the region was invaded by a string of foreign powers. The Assyrians, the Babylonians, and the Persians all had turns controlling Jordanian lands. In 331 BCE, the Persians were defeated by the Greek leader Alexander the Great. After Alexander's death, Greek leaders of the Seleucid dynasty commanded what is now northwestern Jordan for the next three hundred years.

To the south, the Nabataeans, people from the desert, established their own civilization based around their capital of Petra. The Nabataeans became wealthy from tolls levied on traders traveling through their lands. The traders' caravans carried valuable materials such as frankincense and myrrh from Arabia to areas to the north. Nabataea remained independent of Greece, though it was greatly influenced by Greek culture.

Romans, Muslims, and Crusaders

In the first century BCE, the area that is now Jordan came under the control of the vast Roman Empire. The region prospered under Roman rule. The Romans built many roads and

The Pink City of Petra

In a remote valley in southern Jordan lies the country's greatest wonder—the ancient city of Petra. This city was built by the Nabataean people. Petra was at its height from the first century BCE to the first century CE. Wealthy from trade, the Nabataeans created great monuments at Petra, many of which still stand today.

The grandest structures at Petra were carved out of sandstone cliff faces. The sandstone is colored pinkish red, which is why Petra is sometimes called the Pink City. Now a symbol of Jordan, the building known as the Treasury is Petra's most famous landmark. Standing some 130 feet (40 m) high, the Treasury has tall columns modeled after those found in ancient Greek architecture.

After Petra declined, the city was forgotten by everyone but the Bedouin people who traveled through its ruins. In 1812, a Swiss explorer named Jean Louis Burckhardt, disguised as a Bedouin, found his way to the city and sketched its monuments. Intrigued by Burckhardt's descriptions and drawings, many more European adventurers sought out Petra. Since the 1980s, the government of Jordan has actively encouraged foreign travelers to make the trek there. The Pink City now welcomes hundreds of thousands of tourists each year.

buildings. The Temple of Artemis and other Roman ruins at the town of Jarash date from this period.

In 324 CE, the Roman emperor Constantine made Constantinople (now Istanbul, Turkey) the capital of the eastern portion of the Roman Empire. Its construction on the old Greek settlement of Byzantium ushered in the Byzantine period. During this time, Christianity was introduced to Jordan. Many churches were built there, some of which were decorated with elaborate mosaics. The city of Madaba is particularly known for its Byzantine churches.

In 636, armies led by Abu Bakr arrived at the Yarmouk River. They defeated the Byzantines and took control of the

The mosaics at Madaba have many different subjects. This dog chasing a hare dates from the late 500s CE.

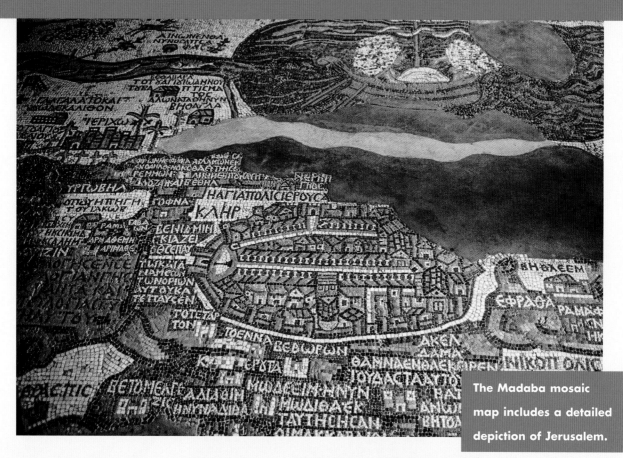

The Madaba mosaic map includes a detailed depiction of Jerusalem.

Madaba's Mosaics

Madaba is nicknamed the City of Mosaics for good reason. In its old homes, buildings, and churches, there are hundreds of mosaics—artworks made by arranging different colored stones into pictures. Many of these images date from the fifth and sixth centuries CE.

The city's mosaics include pictures of everyday life. Some show farmers and fishermen at work. Other mosaics depict the region's plant and animal life. In one, a lion is shown chasing a gazelle. In another, a young boy shows off his pet parrot. Gods and goddesses of Greek myths are also favorite subjects of Madaba mosaics.

The most spectacular mosaic in the city is on the floor of the Greek Orthodox Church of St. George. It was built in the late nineteenth century on the site of a sixth-century church that had been destroyed by an earthquake. In the rubble, a great masterpiece was discovered. It is the oldest known map of the Middle East.

Originally, the famous Madaba mosaic map measured about 20 feet (6 m) by 50 feet (15 m) and included two million stones. It is extremely detailed, with more than 150 place-names noted in Greek. The map has helped archaeologists locate important ancient sites long buried underground.

area. Abu Bakr and his troops were Muslims, followers of the religion of Islam. Islam was based on the teachings of the prophet Muhammad, who had died only four years earlier. Ever since the Battle of Yarmouk, what is now Jordan has been dominated by Muslims of Arab ancestry.

Jordan became part of a series of empires established by families of Islamic rulers. They included the Umayyad, Abbasid, and Fatimid dynasties. They also ruled Jerusalem, considered a holy city by Christians. In 1095, the Pope, the leader of the Roman Catholic Church, called for armies of European Christians to seize Jerusalem from its Muslim rulers. The Christians' military campaigns were called the Crusades.

Uniting the Arab people, a Muslim ruler named Saladin succeeded in driving out the Crusaders in 1187. His Ayyubid dynasty ruled until 1250, when the Mamluks defeated the empire. Jordan remained under Mamluk command until 1517, when the Ottoman Turks took over. The Ottoman Empire, based in Turkey, controlled much of southeastern Europe and western Asia. Under the Ottoman Empire, Jordan languished, virtually ignored by its new rulers.

OTTOMAN EMPIRE

EUROPE

Black Sea

Constantinople

Caspian Sea

ASIA

Mediterranean Sea

AFRICA

Red Sea

KEY
- Ottoman Empire, 1326
- Territory gained by Ottomans, 1326–1362
- Territory gained by Ottomans, 1362–1481
- Territory gained by Ottomans, 1481–1566
- Present-day Jordan

The Arab Revolt

Not until the early twentieth century did the Ottomans start paying attention to the region. In 1908, they completed the Hejaz Railway that ran straight through present-day Jordan. The railway was built to carry Muslim pilgrims to and from the holy city of Mecca, which is farther south on the Arabian Peninsula, in what is now Saudi Arabia. The Ottomans also wanted a way to transport troops quickly. They were concerned that Europeans, particularly the British and the French, were eyeing their lands, where oil had been discovered.

To build the Hejaz Railway, workers had to cut through hard rock.

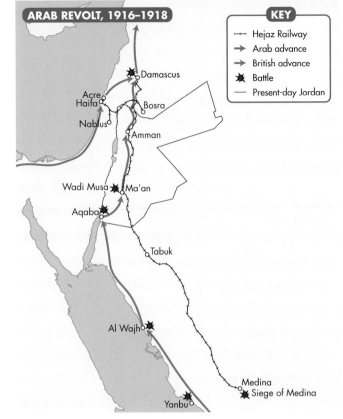

In 1914, World War I broke out. The Ottomans sided with the Germans, who were enemies of the French and British. The British army decided to attack the Ottomans by encouraging their Arab subjects to rise up in revolt. In the past, Arabs had been members of many different tribes, but they had recently begun to think of themselves as a single united people.

With British support, Hussein bin Ali led the Arab Revolt in 1916. He was a member of the Hashemite dynasty, which had long ruled Mecca. His sons Abdullah and Faisal were military leaders in the battle against the Ottoman Turks. In October 1918, Faisal led his army into Damascus, Syria, marking the end of Ottoman rule in the region.

Creating a Nation

During the Arab Revolt, the British had told the rebels that they supported an independent Arab state. But in the peace negotiations in 1919, the British did not follow through on that intent. The French and the British had made a secret agreement back in 1916. It was a plan to divide Arab territory into several areas that the French and the British would then control. Syria and

Lebanon were to be administered by the French. Iraq, Palestine, and Transjordan (the area on the eastern side of the Jordan River across from Palestine) were to be administered by the British.

Abdullah, the son of Hussein, became the emir, or prince, of Transjordan. He named the small town of Amman its capital. Transjordan was in name an independent nation, but the British still controlled its government. British military officers were also in charge of the Arab Legion, Transjordan's army.

After years of negotiation, Transjordan became fully independent in 1946 with Abdullah as its king. Soon thereafter, the country's formal name was changed to the Hashemite Kingdom of Jordan.

The Arab-Israeli War

Meanwhile, a crisis was brewing in Palestine, which lay directly west of Jordan. For decades, Jewish people had been immigrating to Palestine. Following World War II (1939–1945), during which millions of Jews were murdered in Europe, this Jewish immigration increased, angering the local Arab population. The United Nations (UN), an international peacekeeping organization, considered a plan to divide Palestine into two states—one for Jews and one for Arabs. But Arab leaders rejected this plan.

On May 14, 1948, Jewish leaders declared that Palestine was now the independent Jewish state of Israel. The action sparked the Arab-Israeli War. Forces from Transjordan and four other Arab countries (Lebanon, Syria, Iraq, and Egypt) invaded Israel. The fighting continued for months, until the United

Nations finally negotiated a cease-fire in 1949. As part of the deal, King Abdullah gained control over eastern Jerusalem and the West Bank, an area of land just west of the Jordan River.

Palestinians Arrive

Jordan saw a flood of immigrants after the war. Many Palestinians in Israel fled to nearby Jordan. The Palestinian immigrants put a strain on Jordan's economy. They also some-

Arab tanks and trucks line up along the border of Israel in advance of the Arab-Israeli War.

times clashed with the country's elite class, which was loyal to the king. On July 20, 1951, a young Palestinian assassinated King Abdullah in Jerusalem. He also shot at the king's grand-son Hussein, but the bullet bounced off a medal on his chest.

After Abdullah's death, his son Talal became king. But because of illness, he was forced to step down in 1952. The throne then went to Hussein. He formally accepted the crown the next year at the age of seventeen.

The Six-Day War

Hussein faced many challenges as the new king. Unlike some nearby countries, Jordan had little oil, so it was much poorer than other nations in the region. As Hussein tried to improve the economy, he became friendly with wealthy Western nations, particularly the United States, that could provide financial aid to Jordan. These measures angered some people in Arab countries that were opposed to Western influence in the Middle East.

But Hussein's biggest problem was Israel. Many Palestinian Arabs desperately wanted to reclaim their homeland. At an

Young King Hussein waves to his subjects in 1956.

Arab summit in Egypt in 1964, they formed the Palestinian Liberation Organization (PLO). The PLO staged attacks on Israel, and Israel responded with further violence.

The ongoing conflict finally exploded into war in June 1967. Jordan joined with Egypt and Syria to battle Israel. The brief Six-Day War ended with a crushing defeat for Jordan. It was forced to surrender control over eastern Jerusalem and the West Bank, which Israel now occupied. Losing its portion of Jerusalem and its holy sites was a blow to Jordan's tourism industry. But the loss of the West Bank was even worse. The area contained some of Jordan's best farmland. And because Jordan is mostly desert, the West Bank represented about one-half of the territory within Jordan where large numbers of people could comfortably live.

The defeat infuriated some Palestinians in Jordan. They no longer believed that Hussein was capable of wresting Palestine from Israel. Palestinian militants tried to assassinate Hussein and openly defied his army. Clashes between the army and the militants turned into civil war in 1971. The army won the conflict, but not before thousands of people were killed during what became known as Black September.

The Era of King Hussein

For the rest of his reign, Hussein was able to keep Jordan politically stable. He was adept at foreign policy, even in tense times, such as during the Persian Gulf War of the early 1990s. The conflict pitted the United States against Iraq after Iraqi troops had invaded the small country of Kuwait. Despite

Queen Noor (left) and Queen Rania (right) are among the most prominent women in the Middle East.

Two Queens

In some Middle Eastern countries, women have fewer rights than men. Jordan, however, has a fairly strong record on women's rights. Part of the credit goes to its two most recent queens—Queen Noor and Queen Rania.

Queen Noor was born Lisa Halaby, an Arab-American raised in the United States. She studied architecture and urban planning at Princeton University in New Jersey. In 1978, she became the fourth wife of King Hussein and took the name Queen Noor. She worked to better the lives of Jordan's women through the Noor al Hussein Foundation. Other issues she took on included poverty, health reform, and children's welfare. Queen Noor also became the public face of Jordan at many international forums.

Rania Al-Yassin married Abdullah, the son of Hussein, in 1993, six years before he ascended to the throne. Queen Rania has become a model of a modern Jordanian woman. She embraces both traditional Islamic culture and the new ways of a rapidly changing country. Queen Rania has promoted educational opportunities for women and the extension of microcredit, small loans that help women start businesses.

U.S. president Bill Clinton looks on as Israeli prime minister Yitzhak Rabin (left) and King Hussein of Jordan (right) shake hands after signing a peace treaty at the White House in Washington, D.C., in 1994.

pressure from the United States, Hussein followed the will of his people and stayed out of the conflict.

Hussein also negotiated a peace treaty with Israel in 1994, ending a decades-long state of war. The two countries have since been able to work together on some issues, such as security and access to water sources.

At home, the king initiated reforms to make Jordan more democratic. He lifted a ban on political parties. He also oversaw several elections, in which voters were allowed to choose some of their lawmakers.

When Hussein died in 1999, he was well-regarded both inside and outside of Jordan. More than fifty heads of state from foreign governments attended his funeral.

Into the Twenty-First Century

Hussein's successor—his eldest son Abdullah—has largely followed his father's example. He has tried to steer clear of international conflicts while slowly reforming Jordan's internal political system. In the past, the monarchy gathered support through patronage—giving gifts and favors to powerful people. King Abdullah II pledged to make the government less prone to corruption, but critics complain that he has not done enough.

Abdullah II has also worked to modernize Jordan's economy. He has embraced trade deals and other economic reforms in hopes of improving his people's living standard. To bolster the economy, Abdullah II has also tried to strengthen ties with wealthy countries like the United States and the United Kingdom. Some people in Jordan, however, denounce Abdullah for being too beholden to Western powers.

The greatest struggle Jordan faces, however, is maintaining stability in an increasingly volatile Middle East. In the twenty-first century alone, it has had to deal with an invasion of Iraq led by the United States; the overthrow of governments in Egypt, Yemen, and Libya; and the civil war in Syria. The latest of many challenges during Abdullah's reign has been finding a way to absorb more than one million Syrian refugees into Jordanian society.

CHAPTER 5

King and Constitution

I N EARLY 2012, A PROTEST MOVEMENT KNOWN AS THE Arab Spring moved like a wildfire, enflaming countries throughout the Middle East. The movement began in Tunisia, a nation in North Africa, in December 2011, as activists took to the streets, demanding a more democratic government. The protests then quickly spread to Egypt, Libya, Syria, Yemen, Saudi Arabia, and Bahrain. In several countries, Arab Spring led to chaos, as tyrannical governments met the calls for reform with violence.

The people of Jordan also joined the movement. On January 14, 2011, about fifteen thousand Jordanians marched during the Day of Rage—the largest protest in the history of the country. The Jordanian Arab Spring continued for months. But in time, the protests in Jordan petered out. The country saw little violence, but also little change.

Opposite: **In Jordan, military bands include bagpipes, an ancient Middle Eastern instrument. The earliest evidence of bagpipes is a sculpture that dates back three thousand years.**

There are several reasons that the Arab Spring movement did not transform Jordan. The government's tight control over the media and the restraint of its security forces played a role. Also, Jordan's protests were never as heated as protests in other countries.

The protesters were calling for a variety of reforms—from lowering fuel prices to ending government corruption. But few wanted to see their government overthrown. Many Jordanians largely support the government as it stands. It has given them decent housing, accessible health care, and good roads. But even more important, it has largely kept them out of violent conflicts that have destroyed other nearby nations.

In 2011, protesters filled the streets of Amman, calling for government reform.

King Abdullah II walks past a military guard.

Long Live the King!

Adopted in 1946, the national anthem of Jordan is titled "As-salam al-malaki al-urdoni," or "Long Live the King of Jordan." A short, four-line version is played at most public events. But on January 30, when the nation observes the birthday of Abdullah II, Jordanians sing a long version to celebrate the current king and all he has done for his people.

Arabic lyrics	English translation
A-Sha-al Maleek	Long live the king!
A-Sha-al Maleek	Long live the king!
Sa-Mi-yan-ma-qa mu-hu	His position is sublime,
Kha-fi-qa-tin fil ma-ali a-lam m-hu	His banners wave in supreme glory.

The King's Role

Jordan is a constitutional monarchy. The current monarch, King Abdullah II, must govern according to the rules set out in Jordan's constitution, which was adopted in 1952. However, the constitution gives him broad powers over all three branches of government. These branches are the executive, the legislative, and the judicial.

National Government of Jordan

Executive Branch

King

Prime Minister

Cabinet

Legislative Branch

National Assembly

Senate
(65 members)

Chamber of Deputies
(130 members)

Judicial Branch

Court of Cassation

Administrative Court of Justice

Courts of Appeal

Courts of First Instance

Magistrate's Courts

The king is the head of the executive branch. He appoints the prime minister, who is in charge of running the national government's day-to-day operations. The prime minister is also responsible for choosing the members of the cabinet, although the king has to approve the selections.

The cabinet is made up of officials called ministers. Each minister heads a ministry, or department, that deals with one area of government, such as finance, labor, transportation, health, the environment, and information and communication technology.

A Vibrant Capital

Before Amman was named Jordan's capital in 1921, it seemed well past its heyday. It was then a small village, with only a few scattered ruins to suggest its past importance to long-gone civilizations.

Today, Amman is Jordan's leading commercial and cultural center. It is a vibrant city with a growing and ever-changing population of more than 1.2 million people. For many residents, Amman is a beloved refuge from the violence that made them flee from their native countries. In fact, the majority of Ammanis hail from another land, such as Palestine, Iraq, or Syria.

Amman is located in northwestern Jordan.

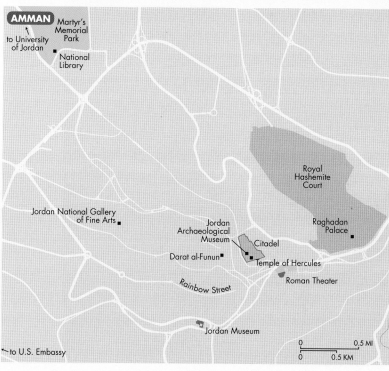

On a hill high above the city center is the Citadel. Visitors can see preserved ruins from the Roman, Byzantine, and Islamic empires that once ruled Jordan. Among the most impressive are the columns of the Temple of Hercules. They were built by the Romans more than two thousand years ago.

Close to the Citadel is the Jordan Archaeological Museum. Other cultural institutions found in Amman include the National Library and the Jordan Museum. Modern artists gather at Darat al-Funun, which houses workshops and galleries. Amman is also a center for education. The University of Jordan in Amman is considered one of the best universities in the Middle East.

In downtown Amman, outdoor markets called souks are always buzzing with activity. Crowds also flock to Rainbow Street. Young people are especially drawn to its trendy shops, busy cafés, and packed clubs.

The Legislature

National laws in Jordan are made by the National Assembly. It has two houses, the Senate and the Chamber of Deputies. The Senate has sixty-five members, and the Chamber of Deputies has 130. Fifteen seats in the Chamber of Deputies are reserved for women, nine for Christians, and three for members of the Chechen and Circassian minority groups. Members of both houses in the National Assembly serve terms of four years.

The king has a great deal of power over the National Assembly. He appoints all of the members of the Senate.

Jordanian legislators gather for a vote.

Wafa Bani Mustafa is a women's rights activist and member of the Chamber of Deputies.

A Champion for Women's Rights

Lawmaker Wafa Bani Mustafa is devoted to improving the lives of the women of Jordan. Born in 1979, Mustafa grew up in the historic town of Jarash. While a student, she ran for office in her school's student council. Mustafa went on to become a lawyer serving female crime victims.

In 2010, at age thirty-one, Mustafa decided to enter politics. She became the youngest member in Jordan's Chamber of Deputies. Outspoken and determined, she fought to persuade her male colleagues to make sexual harassment a crime. She also pushed to amend a law so that children with a Jordanian mother and non-Jordanian father could become citizens of Jordan.

In 2017, Mustafa won her greatest legislative victory. After a three-year battle, she brought about the repeal of a particularly harmful law. The law had shielded men who committed sexual assault from punishment if they married their victims. After this success, Mustafa became only more dedicated to the cause of women's rights. "I am a fighter," she declared. "I don't stop."

The king can dismiss the National Assembly at any time he chooses. He can also veto, or reject, any law passed by the National Assembly. However, the assembly can override a

A woman from Amman shows her ink-stained finger after voting. In Jordan, a person's finger is dipped in ink after voting to show that he or she has already cast a ballot.

veto if two-thirds of the officials in both houses vote to do so.

The people of Jordan elect the members of the Chamber of Deputies. Anyone who is at least eighteen years old can cast a ballot. In recent elections, however, turnout has been low. Some people did not bother to vote because they do not think the Chamber of Deputies has much power. Others claimed the elections were rigged. The election rules ensured that the candidates friendliest to the king were chosen. Palestinian Jordanians, who tend to be less supportive of the monarch, were particularly suspicious of these elections.

In 2016, numerous reforms were put in place to answer these criticisms. But the election that year did not lead to any real changes in the Chamber of Deputies. The turnout was low, with only 37 percent of eligible voters participating. Political parties opposed to the king did not win many seats. This was in part because the new election rules were announced so late that these parties did not have time to organize their campaigns.

Justice and the Courts

The executive branch has great influence in the judicial branch of government because the king has the power to appoint and dismiss judges. The Higher Judicial Council, however, helps in making these decisions.

Criminal and civil cases are tried within the civil court system. Most are brought before a magistrate's court, but important

Supporters of the Islamic Action Front (IAF) wave flags at a rally. The IAF is the largest opposition party in Jordan's Chamber of Deputies.

The Jordanian Flag

The elements of the flag of Jordan honor several different periods and events in the nation's past.

The flag features three horizontal bands. The top one is black, the middle band is white, and the bottom one is green. These bands symbolize three historic dynasties of Arab rulers—the Umayyads, the Abbasids, and the Fatimids. On the flag's left side is a red triangle that overlaps the horizontal bands. It represents the Hashemite family. Hashemite kings have ruled Jordan since 1921. In the middle of the triangle is a seven-pointed white star. It honors Islam, the official religion of Jordan. The seven points stand for the first seven verses in the Qur'an, the holy book of Islam.

Adopted in 1922, the design and colors of Jordan's flag were inspired by banners waved during the Arab Revolt. Modern Jordan has its roots in this 1916 rebellion, during which Arab armies under Hashemite rule fought for their independence from the Ottoman Empire.

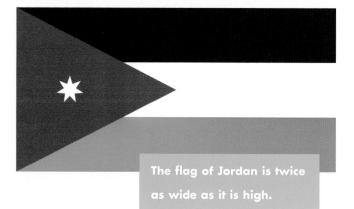

The flag of Jordan is twice as wide as it is high.

cases are decided in the courts of first instance. Challenges to judges' rulings are taken to the Courts of Appeal. Disputes between individuals and government agencies are heard by the Administrative Court of Justice. The highest court in the land is the Court of Cassation, or Supreme Court.

Jordan has two other court systems. Its religious court system is mostly made up of Sharia courts, which enforce Islamic law. There are also separate religious courts for non-Muslims. The cases before religious courts generally deal with personal issues, such as divorce, child custody, and inheritances.

The State Security Court recently replaced Jordan's old military court system. The court tries not just military personnel but also civilians accused of threatening Jordan's security.

Since the Arab Spring demonstrations, the government has sometimes used the court to protect the monarchy. It has punished peaceful protesters on trumped-up charges to discourage anyone else from taking to the streets and demanding change.

Regional Government

Jordanian voters also select the council members of their governorate. The country is divided into twelve governorates, which are similar to states or provinces. Each council works alongside a governor, who is the governorate's leading official. Governors are recommended by the Minister of the Interior, but formally appointed by the king.

Jordanian soldiers help Syrian refugees at the border.

CHAPTER 6

The Jordanian Economy

OR A MIDDLE EASTERN NATION, JORDAN IS FAIRLY stable politically. Its economy, however, is not very stable. As a small country made up mostly of desert lands, it has very little territory where people can comfortably live. It also lacks the natural resources that have made some of its oil-rich neighbors wealthy. As a result, Jordan has some of the highest poverty and unemployment rates in the region.

Opposite: **All different kinds of beans and nuts are for sale at markets in Jordan.**

Farming and Fishing

With little land suitable for growing crops, farming is a very small part of Jordan's economy. Only about 3 percent of its workforce is employed in agriculture.

The country's best farmland is found in the Jordan River valley. There, farmers grow tomatoes, cucumbers, strawberries, and melons in irrigated fields. The area also has orchards of fruit and olive trees. Some crops, particularly wheat and barley, are grown in the highlands.

Many farmers raise livestock, including cattle, chickens, and sheep. Bedouin people in the desert also care for herds of sheep and goats, which provide them with milk and meat. Traditionally, camels were important to the Bedouin for their meat and hides as well as for being a form of transportation.

The fishing industry is tiny in Jordan. There are few fish in its rivers and none at all in the Dead Sea. Fishing in the country is largely confined to its small bit of coastline along the Gulf of Aqaba.

What Jordan Grows, Makes, and Mines

Agriculture (2016)

Tomatoes	837,000 metric tons
Cucumbers	280,000 metric tons
Potatoes	274,000 metric tons

Manufacturing (2016, value of exports)

Chemical products	$2,870,000,000
Clothing	$1,980,000,000
Machinery	$514,000,000

Mining (2013)

Limestone	2,000,000 metric tons
Phosphate	1,728,000 metric tons
Potash	1,046,000 metric tons

RESOURCES

SYRIA

IRAQ

Irbid

Wheat

West Bank

Grapes

Fe

Zarqa

P

Russeifa

Wadi as Sir

Amman

Gyp

ISRAEL

Wheat

K

Gyp

Br

Goats

P

P

Wheat

P

Camels

SAUDI ARABIA

KEY

Cereals

Intensive agriculture

Olives and grapes

Uncultivated desert

Br Bromine

Fe Iron

Gyp Gypsum

K Potash

P Phosphate

Oil

Mining and Manufacturing

Although not rich in oil, Jordan does have some valuable mineral resources. The most important are phosphate and potash, which are used to make fertilizer. Other minerals mined in Jordan include limestone, feldspar, gypsum, marble, and salt. In recent years, deposits of copper and uranium have also been discovered.

About 20 percent of Jordanian workers hold jobs in manufacturing. The country's factories are largely concentrated around Amman. These factories make a variety of goods, including clothing, shoes, fertilizer, medicines, and food products. The government is working to make Jordan a regional center of the high tech industry. Now dependent on foreign oil, Jordan is also looking to develop new sources of energy. It is particularly interested in persuading companies to build wind and solar power plants that will produce electricity without polluting the environment.

Service Industries

Most people in Jordan make a living in the service industry. They include workers in education, health care, trade, transportation, and retail sales. The biggest employer in Jordan is the government. Nearly half of all workers are employed by government agencies or by the military.

Money Facts

The basic unit of currency in Jordan is the Jordanian dinar. But shopkeepers and waiters are likely to ask people for a certain number of *jaydees* when they pay their bill. The slang term comes from the common abbreviation used for the Jordanian dinar—JD.

Jordan produces banknotes worth 1, 5, 10, 20, and 50 dinars. On the front of the bills are portraits of rulers from the Hashemite dynasty. The current king, Abdullah II, appears on the 50-dinar note. On the other side of most bills are pictures of historical landmarks, such as the Ma'an and Raghadan palaces. The writing is in Arabic on the front of the banknotes and in English on the back.

One dinar is worth 100 piastres or 1,000 fils. Prices are usually written in dinars and fils. For instance, a price of 8,750 means 8

King Hussein appears on the front of the 1-dinar note.

dinars and 750 fils. Coins are issued in five denominations: 1, 5, and 10 piastres and ¼ and ½ dinars. In 2018, 1 Jordanian dinar equaled $1.41, and $1.00 equaled 0.79 dinars.

Tourism is another important service industry. Jordan has worked hard to promote itself as a vacation destination. More than four million tourists visit Jordan each year. Most are from Middle Eastern countries.

Jordan's biggest attractions are the ancient city of Petra and the Roman ruins at Jarash. Other draws include the beaches along the Gulf of Aqaba and the spa retreats near the Dead Sea. Increasingly, Jordan is also becoming a center for medical tourism. People from other countries travel there not only to see the sights, but also to receive quality medical treatment at a bargain price.

Seeking Outside Aid

Despite the government's efforts, industries in Jordan are not expanding fast enough to provide employment to everyone who wants a job. Many people, particularly those with college degrees, have to leave Jordan to find work. They might go to another Middle Eastern nation or even farther to a country in Europe or North America. Often, these Jordanian workers send money to their families back home. This money, known as remittances, is not just important to individual family budgets. Remittances also account for a large part of Jordan's national economy.

A CT scan is performed on a patient in Amman.

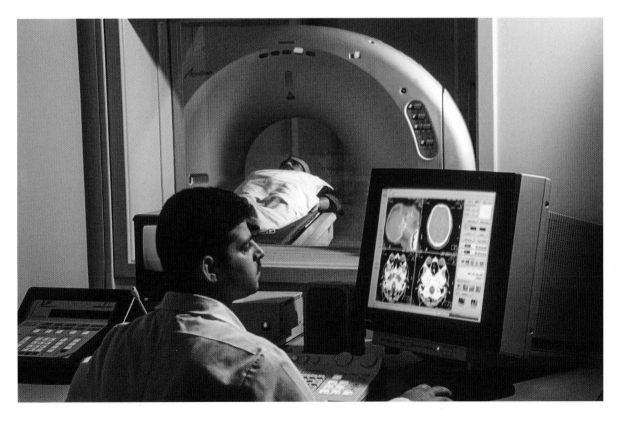

Turning Crafts Into Cash

In Jordan, women earn more college degrees than men. But despite their high educational levels, women make up less than one-fifth of the country's workforce. Old social rules keep women from taking jobs, because they are expected to stay at home and raise children. Women often feel pressured by their husbands, who say they would be ashamed if their wives entered the work world.

But many women, particularly in rural areas, need to work to help support their families. For them, the best employment opportunity is Jordan's growing handicrafts industry. Many organizations train women in traditional crafts and help them sell their work. These women are able to earn a living from home by dividing their time between craft-making and their household duties.

Female artisans make a wide array of goods, including carpets, jewelry, baskets, and embroidered cloth and clothing. They not only bolster their family income. They also help keep these craft traditions alive, preserving an important part of Jordan's cultural heritage.

Weaving is a traditional skill in Jordan.

Another important source of revenue for Jordan is aid from foreign nations. In fact, without this aid, its economy probably could not stay afloat. Some of this money comes from Western allies, particularly the United States. Wealthy Middle Eastern countries, including Saudi Arabia and Kuwait, also contribute a great deal. But the amount of foreign aid Jordan will receive is unpredictable. And even with this assistance, Jordan's national debt now tops $40 billion.

Adding to Jordan's economic woes is the recent flood of refugees from Syria. These refugees are arriving in large numbers, and they are desperately poor. The financial needs of these newcomers threaten to stretch Jordan's already fragile economy to a breaking point. The Syrian refugees have already cost the Jordanian government some $10 billion. Jordan is now asking wealthy nations for even more financial aid to help shoulder the burden of this growing humanitarian crisis.

About eighty thousand people live in the Za'atari refugee camp in northwestern Jordan. The camp is becoming a city, with many children attending school, and thousands of small businesses being started.

CHAPTER 7

The People of Jordan

J ORDAN IS HOME TO JUST OVER TEN MILLION PEOPLE. ITS population is largely young. More than half of Jordanians are under the age of twenty-five. Only about 4 percent are over sixty-five.

The majority of Jordanians live in the country's north-western corner. The southwest along the Gulf of Aqaba is another important population center. Most Jordanians live in cities. Approximately 84 percent of the population lives in an urban area.

Ethnic Backgrounds

Most Jordanians share an ethnicity. Nearly everyone—about 98 percent of the population—is Arab. They trace their ancestry to the Bedouin, the nomadic people who once lived throughout the Middle East's deserts.

Opposite: **The headdresses worn by Bedouin women often feature embroidery or silver decorations.**

Population of Major Cities (2018 est.)	
Amman	1,275,857
Zarqa	792,665
Irbid	307,480
Russeifa	268,237
Wadi as Sir	181,212

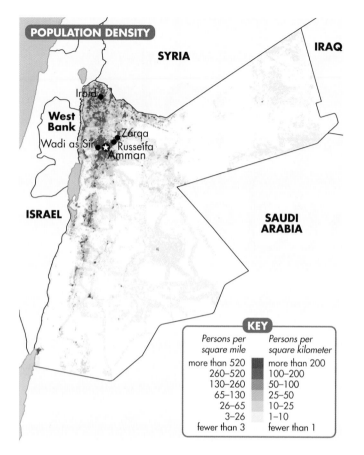

POPULATION DENSITY

SYRIA

IRAQ

Irbid

West Bank

Wadi as Sir

Zarqa

Russeifa

Amman

ISRAEL

SAUDI ARABIA

KEY

Persons per square mile		Persons per square kilometer
more than 520		more than 200
260–520		100–200
130–260		50–100
65–130		25–50
26–65		10–25
3–26		1–10
fewer than 3		fewer than 1

Ethnic Groups

Arab	98%
Circassian	1%
Armenian	1%

Some Jordanians are almost completely of Bedouin heritage. About forty thousand Bedouin continue to dwell in tents in the desert, where they live much as their ancestors did. They keep herds of sheep or goats, moving constantly in search of water and pasturelands for their animals. But most Bedouin no longer live wholly nomadic lives. The government has encouraged them to settle in permanent homes for at least part of the year.

The majority of Jordanian Arabs have a more mixed ancestry. In addition to Bedouin heritage, they are likely to have ancestors from one or more of the numerous foreign peoples who have occupied their lands. For instance, these Jordanians might have Greeks, Persians, or Egyptians far back in their family tree.

Small numbers of people from non-Arab minority groups also live in Jordan. They include Armenians, Kurds, Chechens, and Druze. About 1 percent of Jordanians are Circassian. Their ancestors came to Jordan in the mid-nineteenth century after Russians drove them out of their homeland in the Caucasus region. Circassians have long held important positions in Jordan's government. Since the founding of the kingdom,

Circassian men have served in the royal guard, which protects the monarch's residences.

Palestinians in Jordan

When Jordan was founded in 1946, only about two hundred thousand people lived there. Its population has since exploded. The rise is largely due to Jordan's willingness to take in people from other countries. Some, including large numbers of Egyptians, are guest workers. But many more are refugees from nations plagued by war who have sought a safe home in Jordan.

Circassians perform at a cultural festival in Jarash. About one hundred thousand Circassians live in Jordan.

A large number of refugees came from Palestine. Most arrived in two large waves. The first was in 1948, during the Arab-Israeli War. The second was in 1967, at the end of the Six-Day War. In both cases, Palestinian Arabs immigrated to Jordan from lands that came under the control of Israel.

Jordan granted full citizenship to the Palestinians who arrived directly after the Arab-Israeli war. They and their descendants, therefore, have all the same rights as natives of Jordan. These Palestinians became well integrated into Jordanian society. In some of Jordan's urban areas, Palestinian Jordanians now make up the majority of the population.

A man holds a Palestinian flag at a demonstration in Amman. Most Palestinians in Jordan live in the northern part of the country.

More than a third of Jordanians are younger than fifteen years old.

Who Lives in Jordan?

The government of Jordan conducted a census of its population in 2015. It found that out of 9.5 million people, only 6.6 million were citizens of Jordan. The other 2.9 million living within its borders were people from other countries who had not been granted Jordanian citizenship.

Jordan's Non-Jordanian Population

Syrians	1.265 million
Egyptians	636,270
Palestinians	634,182
Iraqis	130,911
Yemenis	31,163
Libyans	22,700
Others	197,385

Not all Palestinians in Jordan have citizenship, however. Some live in semi-permanent refugee camps run by the United Nations. Many Palestinians are hesitant to put down roots in Jordan because they hope to one day return to their homeland.

Iraqi refugees sit in a coffee shop in Amman. Many of the Iraqis who fled to Jordan to escape war in their country have not been able to return home.

Iraqis and Syrians

In recent decades, many refugees from Iraq have made their way to Jordan. They came to escape the chaos during two wars with the United States—the Persian Gulf War (1990–1991) and the Iraq War (2003–2011). Many of the Iraqi refugees were businesspeople and professionals. The wealth they brought with them was a great benefit to Jordan. The money helped prop up the economy when Jordan could no longer trade goods with war-ravaged Iraq.

Since 2012, Jordan has seen a massive influx of refugees from Syria. They fled a brutal civil war in their home country. Many came by foot over the border, bringing little with them.

Jordan's government says that it has taken in 1.3 million Syrians. About 80 percent of them live in northern towns and cities. The rest are in United Nations' refugee camps. The largest camp, Za'atari, has a population of eighty thousand. Jordan has always prided itself on welcoming foreigners. But the country is now struggling to figure out how to absorb so many impoverished refugees so fast.

Arabic and English

Arabic is the primary language of roughly 290 million people across the world, including nearly all Jordanians. Some Jordanian people belonging to minority groups can also speak their ethnic language. For instance, Circassians in Jordan

A schoolgirl writes Arabic on a board.

might know Adyghe. But they almost always use Arabic in their day-to-day lives.

Classical Arabic is the language of the Qur'an, the holy book of Islam. Modern Standard Arabic developed from Classical Arabic. It is used in most books and newspapers.

Spoken Arabic includes many dialects, or versions. But most Arabic speakers can understand one another. Within Jordan, pronunciation and word choice vary slightly from region to region. How a person says a word might reveal, for example, that they are from Amman in the north or from Aqaba in the south. The two major Jordanian dialects are the Palestinian dialect and the tribal dialect.

The most common second language in Jordan is English. English-speakers are usually people in the middle or upper class. But everyone uses a few English words that have also crept into spoken Arabic. Arabic speakers in Jordan also regularly borrow

Common Arabic Words and Phrases

Al salaam alaykum	Hello
Ma' al-salama	Good-bye
Tisbah ala-khayr (to a man)	Good night
Tisbinin ala-khayr (to a woman)	Good night
Fursa sa'ida	Pleased to meet you
Kif al-hal?	How are you?
Kif al-'a'ila?	How is your family?
Baraka Allah bik	Thank you
Afwan	You're welcome

The Arabic language is written from right to left, the opposite of English.

تعليمات السباحة بالبحر الميت

★ يمنع الغطس

★ عدم السباحة لمسافات طويلة

★ إحم عينيك وفمك من الماء

★ السباحة على الظهر أكثر أماناً

Swimming At The Dead Sea InstructionS

★ Do Not Dive

★ Do Not Swim Far From Shore

★ Protect Eye And Mouth From Watre

★ Try To Swim On Your Back

Writing Arabic

The Arabic alphabet has twenty-eight characters. When Arabic words are transliterated into the Latin alphabet, the alphabet used for written English, they are spelled out using the Latin letters that sound most like the word when it is spoken. Sometimes, however, these sounds can be created in different ways, so Arabic words in the Latin alphabet can have a variety of spellings.

words from the French, Turkish, and Persian languages.

Jordan has a high literacy rate. About 95 percent of Jordanians can read and write. The government provides free literacy classes for all residents of Jordan. But most people learn to read the Arabic language in school as children. Jordan's educational system wants to ensure that all Jordanians are computer literate as well. A recent law requires all students to take a computer studies class in the tenth grade.

CHAPTER 8

Following Islam

JORDAN LIES IN THE PART OF THE WORLD THAT MUSLIMS, Christians, and Jews consider the Holy Land. Several stories told in the Bible occurred within its borders. At Mount Nebo, the Jewish prophet Moses first caught a glimpse of his people's promised land. In the town of Mukawir, the early Christian leader John the Baptist met his death. In the waters of the Jordan River, Jesus himself was baptized.

In contemporary Jordan, however, the most important religion is Islam. More than 97 percent of Jordanians are Muslims, followers of Islam.

The Prophet

Islam was introduced to Jordan in 636 in a dramatic fashion. An army of Muslims led by Abu Bakr met Byzantine troops in a series of battles at the Yarmouk River. After Abu Bakr's

Opposite: **A Jordanian woman kneels on a prayer mat to pray. Muslims always pray facing the direction of Mecca, Saudi Arabia, the holiest city in Islam.**

The Isaiah Scroll is approximately 24 feet (7 m) long. Written in Hebrew, it is a copy of the biblical Book of Isaiah.

The Dead Sea Scrolls

In a cave in 1947, a Bedouin shepherd found some pieces of parchment with strange writing on them. Soon archaeologists discovered more parchment fragments in the area. Eventually, they collected tens of thousands of pieces of ancient parchment. Called the Dead Sea Scrolls, the two-thousand-year-old manuscripts contained copies of Bible verses and other religious texts. For Biblical scholars, they were a treasure trove of information about Jews and Christians in the Holy Land just before and after the birth of Jesus.

The documents were discovered in the West Bank, which was part of Jordan when most of them were found. But in 1967, Israel took over this region. It also seized the Palestine Archaeological Museum, where the Dead Sea Scrolls were housed. Ever since, Jordan has demanded Israel return these historic documents, but Israel has refused. Only a few fragments of the Dead Sea Scrolls remain in Jordan. They are prominently displayed at the Jordan Museum in Amman.

military victory, Islam became the region's dominant religion. At the time, Islam was a new faith. The Prophet Muhammad, the founder of Islam, had died only four years earlier. Born around 570 in what is now Saudi Arabia, Muhammad was a traveling merchant. Muslims believe that when he was about forty, the angel Gabriel came to him. Gabriel is said to have told Muhammad the word of God, or *Allah* in Arabic.

In the city of Mecca, Muhammad preached what he is said to have learned from Gabriel. He told people to abandon their belief in many deities and accept that there is only one true God. His followers collected his teachings, the messages from Gabriel, into the Qur'an. It is the holy book of Islam.

As Muhammad's teachings became more popular, the authorities feared his growing power. Believing they were

Religions of Jordan

Islam	97.2%
Christianity	2.2%
Buddhism	0.4%
Hinduism	0.1%
Other religions	0.1%

A Jordanian man reads the Qur'an.

Muslims are called to prayer five times a day, at dawn, noon, afternoon, sunset, and night. At these times, many devout Muslims stop to pray, regardless of where they are.

planning to assassinate him, Muhammad fled north to the city of Medina in 622. Muhammad's journey from Mecca to Medina is now known as the Hijra.

The Two Branches of Islam

Muhammad continued to preach until his death in 632. Soon afterward, his followers had a dispute over who should be the caliph, the leader of all Muslims. Sunni Muslims said the caliph should be chosen from a group of elite men. Shia Muslims maintained that the caliph had to be a direct descendant of Muhammad himself.

Today, in some Middle Eastern countries, violence has broken out between Sunni and Shiite populations. But Jordan is free of such conflicts, largely because almost all Jordanian Muslims are Sunnis.

A small number of people in Jordan belong to two nontra-ditional sects that grew out of Shia Islam. These are the Druze and the Baha'i religions. Most followers of the Druze faith live in the town of Azraq. Druze diverged from mainstream Shia beliefs in the tenth century. Believers have since hidden their religious practices and teachings from outsiders.

Jordanian members of the Baha'i faith are mostly found in the village of Adassiyeh in the Jordan River valley. The religion was founded in present-day Iran by a man named Baha'u'llah. Baha'is believe that he was the latest in a line of messengers from God that included Muhammad and Jesus.

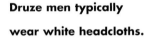

Druze men typically wear white headcloths.

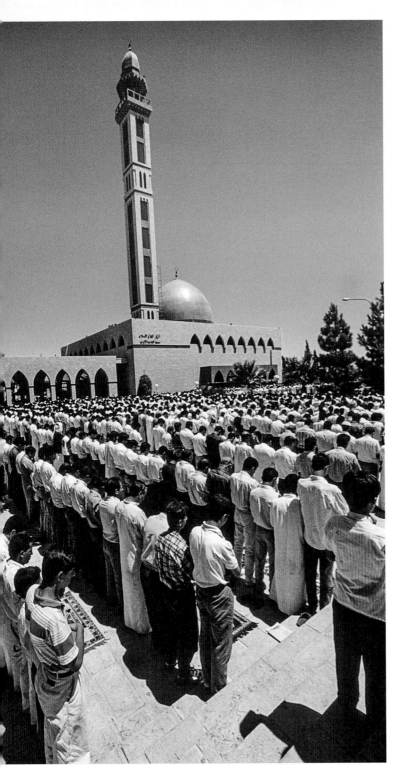

Their spiritual mission is to unify all of humankind and to bring harmony to the world.

Being Muslim

Muslims throughout Jordan and the world observe religious practices known as the Five Pillars of Islam. The first is *shahadah*. It requires Muslims to state their faith by saying, "There is no god but God, and Muhammad is the messenger of God." In Jordan, soon after a baby is born, relatives will whisper these words into the infant's ear.

The second pillar is *salah*. It maintains that Muslims must pray five times a day. The call to prayer is issued from high towers called minarets. They are located in mosques, which are Islamic houses of worship. When Muslims pray, they kneel facing the holy city of Mecca.

Mosques typically have at least one tall tower called a minaret.

The King Hussein bin Talal Mosque is the largest mosque in Jordan. It has room for more than five thousand worshippers.

King Hussein bin Talal Mosque

High atop a hill overlooking the capital of Amman stands Jordan's finest mosque. The King Hussein bin Talal Mosque was built by King Abdullah II to honor his father. The white building is topped by a brown dome and four minarets. The interior has a similarly muted color scheme, with white and cream stone accented by dark wood. The elegant structure is the largest mosque in Jordan.

Zakat, the third pillar, requires Muslims to give money to the poor. The fourth, sawm, obliges them to fast during some religious observances. The fifth and final pillar is hajj. All Muslims who are physically and financially able are expected to travel to Mecca at least once in their lifetime.

Religious Holidays

Jordanian Muslims also observe several religious holidays each year. The longest is Ramadan. It takes place over the ninth month of the Islamic calendar. During the holy month of Ramadan, Muslims do not eat or drink anything during sunlight hours.

The end of Ramadan is celebrated with the feast of Eid al-Fitr. Friends and relatives come together to share the foods and treats they denied themselves the month before.

Another important Muslim holiday is Eid al-Adha, the feast of sacrifice. It is a remembrance of the story of Ibrahim in the Qur'an. When asked by God to kill his son, Ibrahim was

Each evening during Ramadan, Muslims have a meal called *iftar* (breaking of the fast) just after sunset. Often, people gather in large groups for these feasts.

willing to make this sacrifice. God then allowed Ibrahim to kill an animal instead. During Eid al-Adha, families slaughter an animal for a meal that they share with guests. A portion of the meat is also given to the poor.

Two other religious holidays observed in Jordan are Mawlid al-Nabi and Al Isra' wal Miraj. Mawlid al-Nabi is a celebration of the prophet Muhammad's birthday. Al Isra' wal Miraj is a commemoration of Muhammad's night journey to heaven as described in the Qur'an and other sacred texts.

Eid al-Adha is a time of celebration. Many Jordanians take a trip to an amusement park as part of the holiday festivities.

Islam and the Government

Like the daily lives of its people, the government of Jordan is deeply influenced by Islam. The country's constitution names Islam as Jordan's official religion. The government is responsible for managing and funding all Islamic institutions. It pays for the construction of mosques. The government also trains and appoints all imams, the Muslim clergy members who oversee mosques and lead prayers.

Jordan's constitution requires that both the king and his parents be Muslim. Since its founding, all kings of Jordan have been part of the Hashemite dynasty. The family traces its ancestry directly back to Muhammad.

Like earlier kings of Jordan, Abdullah II has vigorously

An imam gives a sermon at a mosque in Amman.

Father Nabil Haddad welcomes visitors to a pilgrimage site in the Jordan River valley.

Promoting Tolerance

Father Nabil Haddad has devoted his life to promoting peaceful relations between people of different faiths. Born in the Jordanian city of Irbid, Haddad is a priest at the Sts. Peter and Paul Melkite Catholic Church in Amman. In 2003, he helped establish the Jordanian Interfaith Coexistence Research Center. The organization advises King Abdullah II as it works to increase understanding between Muslims and Christians in Jordan. The center runs programs for young people and hosts visiting student groups from the United States.

Both in Jordan and abroad, Haddad has also voiced vigorous support for the Amman Message. This address was presented by King Abdullah II and a council of Islamic scholars in 2004. It calls for unity among all Muslims. Meant to challenge the views of Muslim extremists, it also seeks to define Islam as a religion in tune with the ways of the modern world.

championed Islam to the international community. He has promoted Islam as a religion dedicated to peace and has spoken out against terrorist acts committed by Muslim extremists. His government also sponsors the Royal Institute for Inter-Faith Studies. The organization advocates for tolerance between Muslims and people of other religions.

The Greek Orthodox Church of St. John the Baptist stands near the site in the Jordan River valley where it is believed that Jesus was baptized.

Christians in Jordan

Although Islam is dominant in Jordan, the nation's constitution forbids discrimination against religious minorities. However, the government does place some restrictions on non-Muslims. For instance, non-Muslim men cannot marry Muslim women in Jordan. It is also illegal for non-Muslims to try to convert Muslims to their religion.

Almost all non-Muslims in the country are Christians. In fact, Jordan is home to some of the oldest Christian communities in the world. Christians were living in what is now Jordan beginning in the first century CE. Today, Christians make up most of the population in a few towns in northern Jordan.

About half of the Christians in Jordan belong to Orthodox churches, particularly the Greek Orthodox Church. Others are Roman Catholic or Protestant. Protestant groups represented in Jordan include Episcopalians, Anglicans, Evangelicals, Lutherans, Baptists, and Seventh-Day Adventists.

Christians in Jordan are generally treated well by the Muslim majority. Many Christians hold high positions in society and in the government. By law, nine seats in the Chamber of Deputies are reserved for Christian representatives. The Jordanian government also recognizes Easter and Christmas as national holidays. During the Christmas season, Christian towns are decorated with lights and trees. The capital of Amman as well hosts a month-long Christmas market. There, Christians and Muslims come together each year to look at the decorations and shop for handicrafts and treats.

A Roman Catholic priest leads a pilgrimage to the Jordan River. About eighty thousand Catholics live in Jordan.

CHAPTER 9

The Cultural Scene

JORDAN HAS A RICH CULTURAL HERITAGE. ITS traditional art, literature, and music all remain vital and alive, in large part because of the support of the national government. The government also invests heavily in contemporary arts and artists. By doing so, it is working to make Jordan an important cultural hub within the Middle East.

Opposite: **Bedouin jewelry is typically made of silver and colorful beads.**

Handicraft Traditions

Traditional crafts are a big business in Jordan. Today, many artisans make their living by handcrafting items for sale. The goods they produce are particularly popular among tourists who frequent markets and bazaars looking for souvenirs of their time in Jordan.

One such craft tradition is rug making. Bedouin women have long woven goat hair on looms to create rugs and other textiles.

In Jordan, carpets were traditionally used to cover walls, floors, and more.

The rugs helped keep their tents warm on cold desert nights.

As more Bedouin began to settle in permanent villages, rug making was in danger of dying out. But through the Bani Hamida Weaving Project, older women started to teach younger women about the craft. Now women from thirteen communities are employed making rugs. In the past, the rugs usually featured dark oranges, reds, and greens. But more recently, artisans have been experimenting with lighter pastel hues to satisfy customer demand.

The women of Jordan have also long been known for their embroidery skills. Traditionally, a bride before her wedding made special pieces of clothing she would wear throughout her life. She decorated these garments with colorful stitching, often using red thread. Craftspeople now make embroidered dresses, pillows, and purses for the tourist trade.

Other important traditional crafts of Jordan include pottery making, basketry, and glassblowing. Artisans also make jewelry out of gold and silver. Like embroidery, jewelry was an important part of the country's marriage customs. Still today, grooms are expected to present their brides with an expensive piece of jewelry before the wedding takes place. Sometimes the jewelry is in the shape of the hand of Fatima, the daughter of the prophet Muhammad. Such jewelry pieces are said to protect the wearer from harm.

A Jordanian tailor embroiders an Arabic poem onto a dress as part of the decoration.

Making Fine Art

Traditionally, Islamic artists did not depict human beings or animals in their works. Such pictures were thought to go against their religion. Instead, they adorned objects and buildings with geometric designs and with decorative writing called calligraphy.

Some contemporary Muslim artists are reviving the art of calligraphy as part of a movement called *hurufiyya*. This is the use of Arabic letters and words in art. One of the leaders in this movement is the Jordanian artist Wijdan Ali. Her work combines calligraphy with colorful abstract images.

Wijdan Ali poses in front of some of her paintings, which often incorporate calligraphy.

An internationally recognized expert on Islamic art, Wijdan Ali is also the founder of the Jordan National Gallery of Fine Arts in Amman. The National Gallery is one of the largest modern art museums in the Middle East. Its collection includes paintings, sculptures, and photographs by more than one thousand artists from throughout the Arab world.

Also located in the capital is Darat al-Funun, or the Little House of the Arts. Housed in six historic buildings, its galleries feature works by Jordan's most experimental artists. The center also hosts lectures and workshops to introduce the public to the latest currents in Amman's vibrant arts scene.

The National Gallery of Fine Arts is renowned for its modern art.

Writing and Reading

The earliest literature in Jordan was primarily religious texts. One important exception was the *Mu'allaqat*, or the Hanging Poems. Written before Islam was introduced to Jordan, these seven long poems were based on stories long told by Bedouin people.

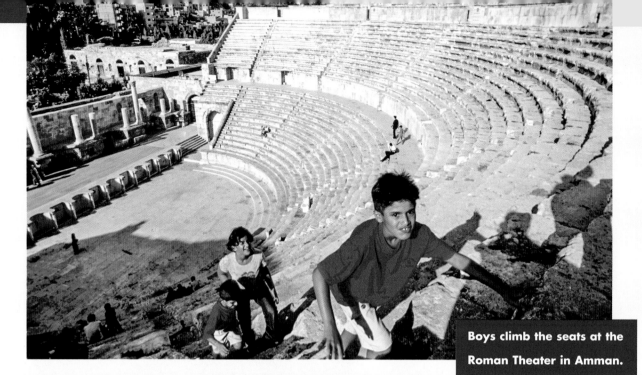

The Roman Theater

In the middle of Jordan's capital of Amman is the massive Roman Theater. It was constructed about two thousand years ago, when the Roman Empire controlled what is now Jordan. Built into a hillside, its seats were arranged in a semicircle facing a stage area.

The original theater could accommodate about six thousand people. It was built with three tiers. The one closest to the stage was reserved for the ruling class. Slightly higher up, the second tier was for soldiers. Up at the top, the third tier was for common people. Even though people in the top tier could barely see the performers on the stage, they could hear them because of the theater's excellent acoustics.

The theater was totally restored in 1957. It is now one of Jordan's leading tourist attractions. Visitors come at sunset to see the ancient structure under a colorful sky. The theater also hosts events and concerts. Every two years, music lovers flock to the theater for al-Balad Music Festival, which showcases young Jordanian musicians as well as bands from neighboring countries.

Jordan did not develop its own literary traditions until the twentieth century. The most famous Jordanian writer is Mustafa Wahbi al-Tal. Popularly known as Arar, he was a poet who called for Jordan to become an independent nation. Every year, a poetry festival is held to honor Arar in his hometown of Irbid.

More recently, many noted Jordanian writers have used their works to examine how their country has changed in modern times. Among them is the novelist Jamal Naji. His acclaimed book *When the Wolves Grow Old* explores the struggles of poor people trying to rise in Jordanian society.

Mustafa Wahbi al-Tal was known for his rebellious, patriotic poems.

A rover drives across Jordan's red desert during the filming of the 2015 movie *The Martian*, which was set on Mars.

Jordan on Film

For many years, the striking landscapes of Jordan have attracted leading filmmakers from around the world. Beginning with the epic film *Lawrence of Arabia* in 1962, a number of big-budget movies have been filmed in Jordan. They include *Indiana Jones and the Last Crusade* and *Transformers: Revenge of the Fallen*. Jordan has also been used as a stand-in for Iraq in several Iraq War dramas, such as *The Hurt Locker*.

Although Jordan has long appeared on film, the country barely had a movie industry until recently. In 2003, the government established the Royal Film Commission. Its mission is to encourage and train Jordanian artists to make their own movies.

Since then, the commission has helped foster the work of new homegrown talents, most notably director Naji Abu Nowar. He won acclaim for his film *Theeb*. It tells the story of a boy struggling to survive in the Jordanian desert during World War I. Abu Nowar developed the film over the course of a year he spent among the Bedouin. In 2016, *Theeb* became the first Jordanian movie to be nominated for the Academy Award for Best Foreign Film.

Another important contemporary writer is Ibrahim Nasrallah, who was born in a Palestinian refugee camp in Jordan. Nasrallah has earned praise for both his poetry and fiction, much of which deals with the difficulties Palestinians face in Jordan. His work has sometimes brought him into conflict with government censors. The government banned a collection of his poetry in 2006 and brought legal charges against him for insulting the state of Jordan. The charges were dropped after the Jordanian Writers Association rallied to Nasrallah's defense.

In 2018, Ibrahim Nasrallah won the International Prize for Arabic Fiction for his novel *The Second War of the Dog*, which is set in a dangerous, futuristic world.

A Jordanian man plays an oud. The instrument does not have a standard number of strings. It typically has between nine and thirteen, usually in pairs.

Song and Dance

The traditional music of Jordan has its roots in the culture of the Bedouin people. Their folk songs, often with improvised lyrics, told heroic tales of family, honor, and love. The songs were usually sung around an evening campfire to the accompaniment of an *oud*. The oud is a stringed instrument similar to a lute. Other traditional instruments played in Jordan include the *mizmar* (a flute), the *tablah* (a drum), the *rababah* (a violin-like stringed instrument), and the *gerbeh* (bagpipes).

The *dabke* is the most popular traditional dance in Jordan. The dancers form a circle, each placing their arms around their neighbors' shoulders. They then stomp the floor with their feet to the rhythm of the music. Today, dancing the dabke is often a part of wedding celebrations. The dabke and

Spreading Peace Through Music

The Jordanian pianist Zade Dirani has played to packed concert halls around the world. But Dirani has always had a much higher ambition than just achieving fame and fortune. Dirani's goal is to play music that will help heal the divisions between people and nations.

Born in Amman in 1980, Dirani learned to play the piano at an early age. He studied music first at Noor Al Hussein's National Music Conservatory in his hometown and then at the Berklee College of Music in Boston, Massachusetts.

After graduating, Dirani began a successful recording career. Eventually he produced five CDs that rose to the top of the New Age charts. Dirani also founded the Zade Foundation for International Peace and Understanding in 2006. He received financial support for the foundation from Jordan's Queen Noor.

Its first program was called The Roads to You: A Celebration of One World. It brought

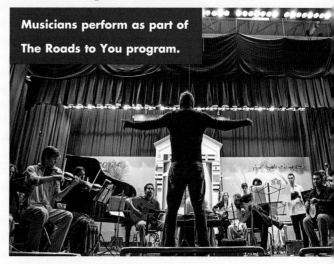

Musicians perform as part of The Roads to You program.

together thirty-five young musicians from twenty countries, many of which were at war. They toured cities in the United States, presenting workshops and concerts. Dirani encouraged the musicians to share their stories with each other and with their audiences. In this way, he hoped to spread understanding between people from different backgrounds.

Another of Dirani's projects was One Night in Jordan: A Concert for Peace. In 2010, he headlined this concert held at Amman's Roman Theater. It also featured forty other musicians from around the world.

In 2016, Dirani was named a regional ambassador to UNICEF. In this role, he has traveled to the Za'atari refugee camp in northern Jordan. There he shared with families of Syrian refugees both his music and his message of tolerance.

Zade Dirani performs at a benefit concert.

other traditional dances are also performed on television by Jordan's national dance troupe.

Young Jordanians fuel the country's lively contemporary music scene. Musicians in Jordan play a wide array of musical styles, including rock, rap, hip-hop, and jazz.

Since 2009, the leading showcase for Jordanian music is al-Balad Music Festival. Held every two years in Amman, it brings big-name bands from other Middle Eastern countries to Jordan. The festival has also helped launch the careers of many local talents. For instance, the alternative rock band El Morabba3 found a large following after appearing at the festival. Combining guitar riffs with the beat of a traditional tablah, El Morabba3 is known for its powerful songs about social and political issues.

A Nation of Soccer Fans

The people of Jordan love playing and watching many different sports, but soccer is by far their favorite. Friends get together for informal games in open spaces and city streets. Many young people also play in soccer clubs organized by the Jordan Football Association.

Soccer enthusiasts watch matches between the twelve teams in Jordan's premier league. For many years, the dominant team in the league has been Al-Faisaly, which is based in Amman. In 2005 and 2006, Al-Faisaly won the international tournament held by the Asian Football Conference. Al-Faisaly's main rival is Al-Wehdat, which is named after a Palestinian refugee camp in Amman.

Other Sports

Other team sports played in Jordan include basketball, volley-ball, and rugby. For individual athletes, boxing and swimming are longtime favorites. Skateboarding and cycling are also becoming increasingly popular with young people.

Martial arts are on the rise as well. That is in part due to the career of Ahmad Abughaush. Jordan has sent athletes to the Summer Olympics since 1980. But the only time a

Jordanians celebrate their national soccer team's triumph in a match.

Jordanian has taken home a medal was during the 2016 Olympics. Abughaush decisively beat all his competitors to win the gold in tae kwon do. After the award ceremony that crowned him Jordan's first Olympic champion, Abughaush said it was "a great feeling to listen to the national anthem of Jordan being played in Rio in front of the whole world."

Traditional sports still enjoyed in Jordan include horse and camel racing. Car racing is also a beloved national pastime, because it is sponsored by the royal family. King Abdullah II himself has competed in the annual Jordan International Rally. Jordanian racers participate in competitions with Middle Eastern countries, such as Qatar, Kuwait, and the United Arab Emirates.

Ahmad Abughaush (in red) won the gold medal in tae kwon do in the 2016 Olympics. Participants in the sport, which began in Korea, score points based upon carefully placed kicks.

Dima (left) and Lama Hattab train in Amman.

Going to Extremes

Since their teens, the Hattab sisters have had something to prove. They want to show their fellow Jordanians that a woman can endure any physical challenge a man can.

Identical twins, Dima and Lama Hattab were born in 1980 in the outskirts of Amman. They were always athletic, and biked and ran around their neighborhood. In school, they were recruited for the track team.

When they were eighteen, the Hattabs entered a half marathon, which stretches 13 miles (21 km). Though the two were used to short races, neither had ever tried long-distance running before. But even without preparation, Lama came in third, and Dima came in fourth. In 2000, Lama won a full marathon of 26 miles (42 km), and Dima took first in a 31-mile (50 km) race.

The idea of a female athlete was new to many Jordanians. Some mocked the Hattab twins, but the sisters just kept looking for new ways to push their bodies to the limits. They have participated in many ultramarathons, including the Marathon des Sables. In this grueling event, runners travel over 156 miles (251 km) of the Moroccan desert over six days. The women also helped organize the Jabal Isrhin Marathon, a charity run held in Wadi Rum in southern Jordan.

Dima and Lama Hattab have also taken up another daring sport—mountain climbing. They hope one day to scale Mount Everest, the world's highest peak.

CHAPTER 10

Living in Jordan

W HEN JORDANIANS GREET A VISITOR, THEY OFTEN say, "*Ahlan wa sahlan.*" The Arabic phrase invites a guest to feel at ease, as though they are part of the family.

This warm greeting displays the spirit of hospitality that is a defining characteristic of the people of Jordan. It also reveals the great value Jordanians place in family ties. To treat visitors like family is to guarantee them the kindness and respect Jordanians always grant their closest relatives.

Family Matters

The social life of most Jordanians is centered on their families. Special occasions and holidays are usually celebrated with relatives. In more traditional families, men and women are separated into different areas during these events.

Opposite: **Serving coffee is an important part of hospitality among the Bedouin of Jordan.**

Hajla is a variation on hopscotch.

Playing Hajla

Children in Jordan, especially those in cities, often fill their free time with television and video games. But sometimes they like to go outside to play traditional games, just like their parents and grandparents did.

Hajla, a version of hopscotch, is a favorite with girls. To begin the game, one player draws a grid of eight squares (four rows of two each). She can make the grid with a piece of chalk on a sidewalk or with a stick in the sand.

Each player starts her turn by tossing a flat rock into the square closest to her. She then must hop into the square on one foot. Using the same foot, she then has to slide the rock and hop into the next square. She continues moving through the grid until the rock or her foot lands on a line. Her turn then comes to an end, and she must hand the rock off to the next player.

Most Jordanian households include several generations of family. Grandparents, parents, and children often live under the same roof. Children sometimes remain in their family home well into adulthood, so they can help care for older relatives.

The type of house a Jordanian family has depends on where they live. The most traditional style of housing is used by the small population of Bedouin who still live as nomads.

Traveling through the desert in search of water, they camp out in tents made of goat hair and sheep's wool.

Settled Bedouin and other rural Jordanians live in small villages. These settlements usually include a cluster of concrete or stone houses along with a mosque and a school. Larger villages might also have a post office, a store, and a coffeehouse.

Amman is a bustling city. Its population more than doubled between 2004 and 2015.

In Jordan, some marriages are traditionally Arab, some are Western, and some are a mix of the two.

Marriage in Jordan

In Jordan, young people generally do not go on dates when they are looking for marriage partners. Instead, they enter into marriages arranged by older people in their families.

Once a couple decides to marry, the two families come together at an engagement party. The groom's family brings sweets to serve with tea and coffee at the bride's home. The groom also presents the bride with an expensive piece of jewelry.

Weddings are elaborate affairs. They include many parties over several days. On the wedding day itself, the groom leads a caravan of cars to pick up the bride. As they all head to the wedding venue, guests celebrate by blasting loud music, honking car horns, and shooting guns in the air.

Usually, before the wedding the bride and groom sign papers that legalize their marriage. The actual wedding can then be devoted to partying. Everyone dances, sings, and feasts on incredible spreads of food.

Wedding guests often number in the hundreds or even thousands. Throwing an appropriate event therefore can cost a huge amount of money. The groom and his family are expected to pay for the wedding. Sometimes, a man will spend years saving up so he can marry. The average age of a Jordanian groom is twenty-nine, one of the highest of any country in the world.

Most Jordanians live in cities. Their homes are most commonly townhouses or apartments. Nearly all have electricity and running water. In the largest urban centers, people have access to all the amenities of European or North American cities. They are full of shopping malls, movie theaters, sports arenas, restaurants, and all the other features of modern city life.

In Fashion

In cities, many Jordanians wear the same type of clothing as people do on the streets of New York City or London, England. Men are dressed in suits or casual shirts and pants. Women wear dresses or blouses with skirts or slacks.

Both Muslim men and women, though, try to dress modestly, as their religion requires. Even on warm days, they wear clothing that keeps their arms and legs out of view. Some conservative women also cover their heads with scarves or their faces with veils.

Many men wear headscarves called kaffiyehs. If they are of Bedouin ancestry, the scarf is often red and white. If they are

A young Bedouin boy wears a headscarf called a keffiyeh. These garments are versatile. They can be used to protect people from the sun, the wind, dust, or cold temperatures.

of Palestinian heritage, it is black and white. A kaffiyeh is held in place by a black rope known as an agal.

In rural areas, people often wear flowing gowns associated with the Bedouin. Other traditional clothing includes elaborately hand-embroidered dresses and tunics. The old town of Salt is known for its unique traditional dresses. Distinguished by their long pointed sleeves, these dresses are made from more than 50 yards (46 m) of fabric. Much of the cloth is draped over a belt to form a huge pocket in the front.

A Tasty Diet

The food of Jordan is a tasty mix that shares flavors with Lebanese, Syrian, and Egyptian cooking. Many dishes feature olive oil, garlic, lemon juice, yogurt, and cumin. Pork is forbidden by Islamic law. But hearty meals in Jordan are full of grilled chicken and lamb, and seafood restaurants abound in Amman and Irbid.

Most Jordanians eat breakfast early in the day. It often includes eggs, cheese, olives, and *khubez* (a type of flatbread). A favorite breakfast dish is *fuul*. It is made of fava beans mashed up with olive oil, lemon juice, and chopped chilies.

Lunch is usually the day's biggest meal. A filling meat or chicken stew served with rice or potatoes is typically on the menu. Dinner is served late, usually after 8 o'clock at night. It might start with a bean or vegetable soup, followed by a serving of meat and bread.

Mansaf is considered the national dish of Jordan. A Bedouin specialty, it is slow-cooked spiced lamb on a bed of

Sipping Sahlab

During the winter, Jordanians enjoy a sweet warming drink called *sahlab*. It became popular throughout the Middle East during the days of the Ottoman Empire.

Traditionally, the drink is made from milk thickened with a powder called sahlab and flavored with rose water, cinnamon, nuts, and coconut. This simple version of this tasty treat does not include the rose water and substitutes cornstarch for the sahlab. If you prefer a smoother texture, though, you can leave the cornstarch out. Have an adult help you with this recipe.

Ingredients
2 cups milk
1 tablespoon cornstarch (optional)
1 tablespoon sugar

Garnishes
1 tablespoon chopped pistachio nuts
1 tablespoon grated coconut
Sprinkling of ground cinnamon

Directions
If you are not using cornstarch, divide the milk into two mugs. Place the mugs in a microwave. Heat on high until the milk is steaming.

If you are using cornstarch, pour the milk into a saucepan. Heat it on the stove until it comes to a boil. Add the cornstarch, and turn the heat down to low. Stir the milk for about ten minutes or until it thickens. Pour the milk and cornstarch mixture into two mugs.

Divide the sugar between the two mugs and stir. (You can use more or less sugar, depending on how sweet you want your drink to be.)

Share your sahlab with a friend. You each can top it with any or all of the garnishes according to your tastes.

Mansaf is made with lamb, rice, yogurt, almonds, and thin bread. Like most foods in Jordan, it is traditionally eaten with the hands.

rice topped with a yogurt sauce. Mansaf takes hours to make. It is usually served only on special occasions, such as birthdays or anniversaries.

Going Out

Jordanians usually have their meals at home. Sitting in a circle, the entire household shares food on large platters placed in the center. When people do go to restaurants, they often start their meal with meze, which are small tastings of food. These might include eggplant dip, chopped liver, spiced olives, and vine leaves stuffed with meat and vegetables.

For a more informal meal out, Jordanians often stop at food stands. These stands sell street snacks like grilled chicken kebabs and falafel, patties of fried chickpeas.

Anyone craving a treat can visit a pastry shop. The desserts are very rich and sweet. One favorite is *kunafeh*, a cheese pastry soaked in sugary syrup. Jordanians also love *baglawa*, layers of pastry dough filled with honey and nuts.

Every town or city neighborhood also has a coffeehouse. In the past, coffeehouses were places where men gathered to talk, play cards, and watch sports on television. But in cities today, many coffeehouses are frequented by women as well as men.

In Jordan, strong coffee is flavored with cardamom and served in little cups. Offering coffee to guests is a way Jordanian hosts show their hospitality. Hosts will keep refilling the cups until their guests tilt the cups from side to side to signal they have had enough.

A food vendor slices kebab meat at an event in Jordan.

National Holidays

January 1	New Year's Day
May 1	Labor Day
May 25	Independence Day
December 25	Christmas Day

Several Muslim holidays are also national holidays. Because the Islamic calendar is eleven days shorter than the Western calendar, the date of these holidays according to the Western calendar varies from year to year.

Mawlid al-Nabi	*Eid al-Adha*
Eid al-Fitr	*Hijri* (Islamic) New Year

Other drinks widely enjoyed in Jordan include tea and fruit juice. Muslims are not permitted to consume alcohol. But Jordanian Christians, especially in the cities of Amman and Madaba, drink arak, a liquor made from aniseed.

Celebrating Jordan

Each year, Jordanians enjoy getting together with friends and family during national holidays. Many, such as Eid al-Fitr and Eid al-Adha, are religious observances. But Jordanians also celebrate several nonreligious holidays. Among them is Labor Day. Every May 1, people get a day off as the nation celebrates the workers who keep the economy going.

June 10 is Army Day. It is a celebration of Jordan's military might. The holiday also commemorates the Arab Revolt of 1916, during which the people of what is now Jordan fought for their independence from the Ottoman Empire. On

Army Day, soldiers march in a great parade in Amman. Military tanks and trucks roll along the parade route as fighter planes fly overhead. Watching the parade is a family event, with many children dressing up in military garb.

Jordanians also take to the streets every May 25 for their country's Independence Day celebration. Everywhere, people wave Jordan's flag, indulge in treats, and listen to musicians and singers performing patriotic songs. At a ceremony at the Raghadan Palace, King Abdullah II bestows medals on distinguished Jordanian scientists, performers, artists, and athletes.

Jordanians gather for an Independence Day celebration.

Independence Day is a time for parties and celebrations. But it is also a chance for Jordanians to reflect on all that they love about their country. In just over seventy years, Jordan has developed into a vibrant nation with a distinct identity. Melding people of different backgrounds and beliefs, it has created a unique culture that respects the old while embracing the new. And one of the things Jordanians most value about their young country is its stability. In a region consumed by war and conflict, they feel grateful that in Jordan they can go about their everyday lives in peace.

Timeline

Jordanian History

ca. 8500 BCE
People begin living in settlements in present-day Jordan.

ca. 1200 BCE
The kingdoms of Ammon, Moab, and Edom emerge in what is now Jordan.

1st century BCE
The Jordan region becomes part of the Roman Empire.

331 BCE
Greek leader Alexander the Great conquers the region.

636 CE
Muslim armies take over the region after their victory in the Battle of Yarmouk.

1187
Saladin unites the Arab people and drives Christian Crusaders from their lands.

1517
The Jordan region becomes part of the Ottoman Empire.

1916
Hussein bi Ali leads th Arab Revol

| 10,000 | BCE 0 CE | 1000 | 1200 | 1400 | 1600 | 1800 | 1900 |

ca. 2500 BCE
The Egyptians build the pyramids and the Sphinx in Giza.

ca. 563 BCE
The Buddha is born in India.

313 CE
The Roman emperor Constantine legalizes Christianity.

610
The Prophet Muhammad begins preaching a new religion called Islam.

1054
The Eastern (Orthodox) and Western (Roman Catholic) Churches break apart.

1095
The Crusades begin.

1215
King John seals the Magna Carta.

1300s
The Renaissance begins in Italy.

1347
The plague sweeps through Europe.

1453
Ottoman Turks capture Constantinople, conquering the Byzantine Empire.

1492
Columbus arrives in North America.

1500s
Reformers break away from the Catholic Church, and Protestantism is born.

1865
The American Civil War ends.

1789
The French Revolution begins.

1776
The U.S. Declaration of Independence is signed.

1917
The Bolshevi Revoluti brings commun to Russi

1914
World War begins.

1879
The first practical lightbulb is invented.

World History

128 *Enchantment of the World* **Jordan**

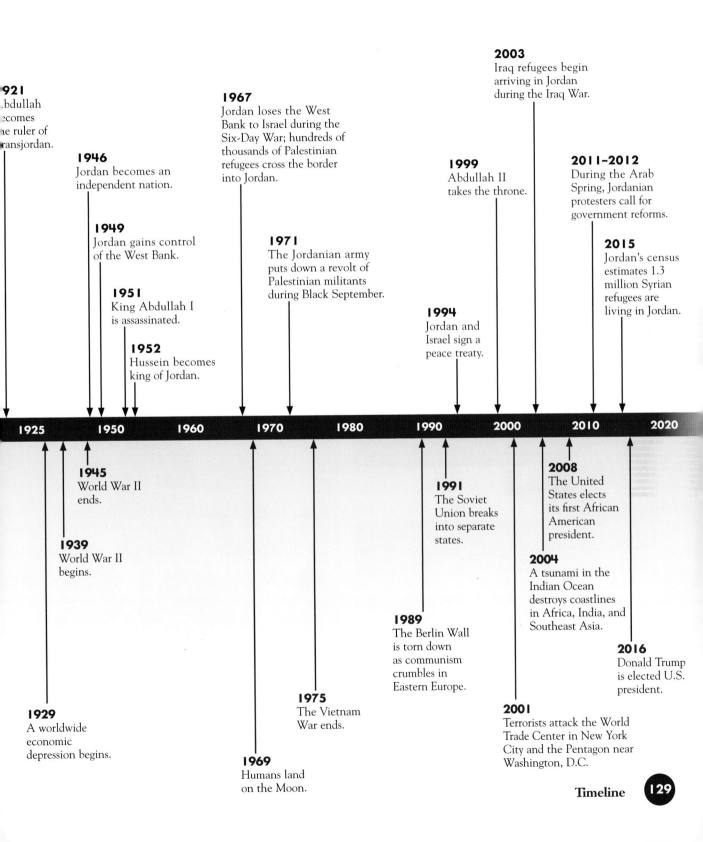

1921
Abdullah becomes the ruler of Transjordan.

1946
Jordan becomes an independent nation.

1967
Jordan loses the West Bank to Israel during the Six-Day War; hundreds of thousands of Palestinian refugees cross the border into Jordan.

2003
Iraq refugees begin arriving in Jordan during the Iraq War.

1999
Abdullah II takes the throne.

2011–2012
During the Arab Spring, Jordanian protesters call for government reforms.

1949
Jordan gains control of the West Bank.

1971
The Jordanian army puts down a revolt of Palestinian militants during Black September.

2015
Jordan's census estimates 1.3 million Syrian refugees are living in Jordan.

1951
King Abdullah I is assassinated.

1994
Jordan and Israel sign a peace treaty.

1952
Hussein becomes king of Jordan.

1925   1950   1960   1970   1980   1990   2000   2010   2020

1945
World War II ends.

1991
The Soviet Union breaks into separate states.

2008
The United States elects its first African American president.

1939
World War II begins.

2004
A tsunami in the Indian Ocean destroys coastlines in Africa, India, and Southeast Asia.

1989
The Berlin Wall is torn down as communism crumbles in Eastern Europe.

2016
Donald Trump is elected U.S. president.

1929
A worldwide economic depression begins.

1975
The Vietnam War ends.

2001
Terrorists attack the World Trade Center in New York City and the Pentagon near Washington, D.C.

1969
Humans land on the Moon.

Fast Facts

Official name:	Hashemite Kingdom of Jordan
Capital:	Amman
Official language:	Arabic
Official religion:	Islam
Year of founding:	1946
National anthem:	"As-salam al-malaki al-urdoni" ("Long Live the King of Jordan")
Government:	Parliamentary constitutional monarchy
Head of state:	King
Head of government:	Prime minister

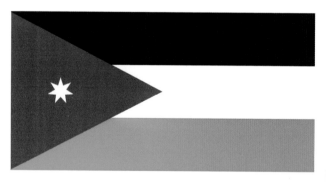

Left to right: **National flag, King Hussein (left) and King Abdullah II**

Floating in the Dead Sea

Area:	34,495 square miles (89,342 sq km)
Latitude and longitude of geographic center:	31°00' N, 36°00' E
Bordering countries:	Israel and the West Bank to the west, Syria to the north, Iraq to the northeast, and Saudi Arabia to the east and south
Highest elevation:	6,083 feet (1,854 m), at Umm ad Dami
Lowest elevation:	1,414 feet (431 m) below sea level, at the Dead Sea
Average high temperature:	In Amman, 55°F (13°C) in January, 90°F (32°C) in July
Average low temperature:	In Amman, 40°F (4°C) in January, 69°F (21°C) in July
Average annual precipitation:	11 inches (28 cm) in Amman

National population (2017 est.):	10,248,069	
Population of major cities (2018 est.):	Amman	1,275,857
	Zarqa	792,665
	Irbid	307,480
	Russeifa	268,237
	Wadi as Sir	181,212

Landmarks:
- ▶ *Church of St. George*, Madaba
- ▶ *Citadel*, Amman
- ▶ *King Hussein bin Talal Mosque*, Amman
- ▶ *Temple of Artemis*, Jarash
- ▶ *Treasury*, Petra

Economy: Jordan's economy is largely focused on service industries, such as education, information technology, and tourism. The government employs about half of all workers. With water in short supply, the only farmable land is found in the temperate northwest. Among Jordan's leading agricultural products are tomatoes, cucumbers, and olives. Minerals mined in Jordan include limestone, potash, and phosphates. With limited farmland and natural resources, Jordan's economy relies heavily on foreign aid, especially from the United States.

Currency: Jordanian dinar. In 2018, 1 Jordanian dinar equaled $1.41, and $1.00 equaled 0.79 dinars.

System of weights and measures: Metric system

Literacy rate: 95%

Common Arabic words and phrases:

Al salaam alaykum	Hello
Ma' al-salama	Good-bye
Tisbah ala-khayr (to a man)	Good night
Tisbinin ala-khayr (to a woman)	Good night
Fursa sa'ida	Pleased to meet you
Kif al-hal?	How are you?
Kif al-'a'ila?	How is your family?
Baraka Allah bik	Thank you
Afwan	You're welcome

Prominent Jordanians:	Abdullah II	(1962–)
	King	
	Ahmad Abughaush	(1996–)
	Tae kwon do Olympic athlete	
	Naji Abu Nowar	(1981–)
	Filmmaker	
	Wijdan Ali	(1939–)
	Artist and art historian	
	Zade Dirani	(1980–)
	Pianist and composer	
	Dima and Lama Hattab	(1980–)
	Marathon runners	
	Hussein	(1935–1999)
	King	
	Mustafa Wahbi al-Tal	(1897–1949)
	Poet	

Clockwise from top: **Currency, Dima (left) and Lama Hattab, young Jordanians**

To Find Out More

Books

▶ Gordon, Matthew S. *Islam*. New York: Chelsea House Publishers, 2009.

▶ *Jordan*. New York: Lonely Planet, 2015.

Video

▶ *The Castles of the Umayyad Desert: Jordan's Historic Legacy*. Tampa, FL: TravelVideoStore.com, 2007.

▶ *NOVA*. "Petra: Lost City of Stone." Arlington, VA: PBS, 2015.

▶ Visit this Scholastic website for more information on Jordan:
www.factsfornow.scholastic.com
Enter the keyword **Jordan**

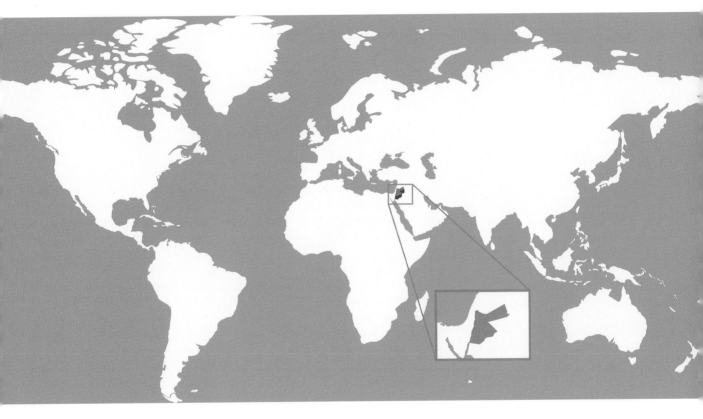

Location of Jordan

Index

Page numbers in *italics* indicate illustrations.

Iraq War, 82
Irbid, 17, 20, 77, 97, 107
Isaiah Scroll, 88
Islam. *See also* religion.
    Abdullah II (king) and, 96–97
    alcohol and, 126
    Al Isra' wal Miraj holiday, 95
    Amman Message, 97
    Baha'i sect, 91
    caliphs, 90
    clothing and, 121
    Druze sect, 91, *91*
    Eid al-Adha holiday, 94–95, *95*, 126
    Eid al-Fitr holiday, 94, 126
    Fatima (daughter of Muhammad), 103
    Five Pillars of Islam, 92–93
    food and, 94, *94*, 95, 122
    government and, 96–97
    hajj (fifth pillar of Islam), 93
    Hejaz Railway and, 46
    Hijra, 90
    holidays, 94–95, 126
    imams, 96, *96*
    introduction of, 87–88
    jewelry and, 103
    Mawlid al-Nabi holiday, 95
    Mecca, 46, 47, 86, 89, 90, 92, 93
    Medina, 90
    minarets, 92, *92*, 93
    mosques, 92, *92*, 93, *93*, 96, *96*
    Muhammad (prophet), 11, 45, 88–90, 95
    national flag and, 66
    prayer, 86, 90, 92
    Qur'an (holy book), 66, 84, 89, *89*, 94–95
    Ramadan (holy month), 94, *94*
    salah (second pillar of Islam), 92
    sawm (fourth pillar of Islam), 93
    shahadah (first pillar of Islam), 92
    Sharia law, 66, 122

Shia Muslims, 90, 91
Sunni Muslims, 90
    women and, 86, 121
    zakat (third pillar of Islam), 93
Islamic Action Front (IAF), 65
Israel, 13, 15, *19*, 21, 24, 25, 48–49, 51, 52, 54, *54*, 80, 88

J

Jabal Isrhin Marathon, 115
Jarash, *38*, 72, 79
jerboas, 31
Jerusalem, 49, 52
jewelry, *100*, 103, 120
Jewish people, 48
John the Baptist, 87
Jordan Archaeological Museum, 61
Jordan Football Association, 112
Jordanian dinar (currency), 72, *72*
Jordanian Interfaith Coexistence
    Research Center, 97
Jordanian Writers Association, 109
Jordan International Rally, 114
Jordan Museum, 61, 88
Jordan National Gallery of Fine Arts, 105, *105*
Jordan Natural History Museum, 20
Jordan River, 15, 16, 19, *19*, 25, 87
Jordan River valley, 15, 17, *17*, 27, 69, 98
judicial branch of government, 60, 65–67

K

kaffiyeh (headscarf), 9, 121–122
khamsin winds, 18, *18*
King Hussein bin Talal Mosque, 93, *93*
kunafeh (food), 125
Kuwait, 75

L

Lake Tiberias. *See* Sea of Galilee.

languages, 72, 83–85, *83*, *85*, *103*
Lawrence of Arabia (film), 22, 108
Lawrence's Spring, 22, *22*
Lawrence, T. E., 22, *22*
Lebanon, 47–48
legislative branch of government, 60, 62–65, *62*
Libya, 55, 57
Libyan people, 81
lions, 37, *37*
literacy rate, 85
literature, 105–107, *107*, 109, *109*, 133
Little House of the Arts, 105
livestock, 28, 39, 70, 78, 119
lizards, 33
"Long Live the King of Jordan" (national
    anthem), 59

M

Madaba, 43, 44, 126
Madaba mosaic map, *44*
Mamluk Sultanate, 45
mansaf (national dish), 122, 124, *124*
manufacturing, 70, 71
maps. *See also* historical maps.
    Amman, *61*
    geopolitical, 8
    Madaba mosaic map, 44, *44*
    population density, *78*
    resources, *71*
    topographical, *16*
Marathon des Sables, 115
marathon running, 115, *115*, 133, *133*
marine life, 21, 33–34, *34*, 36
marketplaces, 61, 68, 99, 101
marriage, 63, 98, 102, 103, 112, 120, *120*
martial arts, 113–114, *114*, 133
The Martian (film), 23, 108
Mawlid al-Nabi holiday, 95
Mecca, Saudi Arabia, 46, 47, 86, 89, 90, 92, 93
Medina, Saudi Arabia, 90

Supreme Court. *See* Court of Cassation.
Syria, 13, 15, 20, 47–48, 52, 55, 57, 61
Syrian people, 55, *67*, 81, 82–83, 111

T

tae kwon do, 114, *114*, 133
Talal (king), 48, 50
television, 93, 112
Temple of Artemis, 43
Temple of Hercules, 61
terrorism, 13, 97
Theeb (film), 108
tourism, 22, 24, 30, *36*, 42, 52, 72, 101,
    102, 106
towns. *See also* cities; villages.
    Azraq, 91
    coffeehouses, 125
    Jarash, *38*, 72, 79
    Mukawir, 87
    Salt, 122
trade, 41, 42, 55, 82
Transjordan, 48
transportation, *46*, 70
Treasury building, 42, *42*
trees, 28, *29*

tribal dialect, 84

U

Umayyad dynasty, 45, 66
Umm ad Dami, 16, 17
United Arab Emirates, 37
United Nations (UN), 48–49, 81, 82
United States, 52, 53, *54*, 55, 75, 82, 111
University of Amman, 61

V

villages. *See also* cities; towns.
    Adassiyeh, 91
    buildings in, 119
    early kingdoms, 39
    rug making and, 102

W

Wadi Araba, 31
Wadi as Sir, 77
Wadi Rum, *14*, 22, 23, 30, 115
Wahbi al-Tal, Mustafa, 106–107, *107*,
    133
water, 22, 24–25, 54, 78, 121
weaving, 74, *74*

West Bank, 15, 49, 52, 88
When the Wolves Grow Old (Jamal Naji),
    107
wildflowers, *26*, *27*, 28
wildlife. *See* animal life; insect life;
    marine life; plant life; reptilian life.
wind power, 71
women, 53, 62, 63, 74, 86, 101–102,
    115, 117, 121, 125
World War I, 47
World War II, 48

Y

Yarmouk River, 19, 43, 87
Yarmouk University, 20
Yemen, 55, 57
Yemeni people, 81

Z

Za'atari refugee camp, *75*, 83, 111
Zade Foundation for International Peace
    and Understanding, 111
zakat (third pillar of Islam), 93
Zarqa, 17, 20, 77
Zarqa River, 19

Meet the Author

L IZ SONNEBORN, A GRADUATE OF SWARTHMORE COLLEGE IN
Pennsylvania, lives in Brooklyn, New York. She has written
more than one hundred books for adults and young readers,
specializing in American and world history and biography. Her books
include *The End of Apartheid in South Africa*, *The Great Irish Famine*,
The Khmer Rouge, *The American West*, *The Great Black Migrations*,
and *A to Z of American Indian Women*. Sonneborn is also the author
of numerous volumes for the Enchantment of the World Series,
including *Iraq*, *Kuwait*, *Yemen*, *Pakistan*, *Tibet*, *North Korea*, *Mexico*,
and *France*.

Photo Credits

Photographs ©: cover: Mint Images/Getty Images; back cover: vintagerobot/iStockphoto; 2: Steve Outram/Robert Harding Picture Library; 4 top left: Andre Seale/VWPics/Redux; 4 top center: Joel Carillet/ Getty Images; 4 top right: Kertu/Shutterstock; 5 left: Yadid Levy/Alamy Images; 5 right: Cultura RM Exclusive/ Kevin C Moore/Getty Images; 6: Cultura RM Exclusive/Kevin C Moore/Getty Images; 11: Maher Attar/Sygma/ Getty Images; 12: Scott Peterson/Getty Images; 14: Jamie Friedland/Getty Images; 17: Ahmad A Atwah/ Shutterstock; 18: liseykina/iStockphoto; 19: Georg Gerster/Panos Pictures; 20 top right: Maciej Dakowicz/ Alamy Images; 20 bottom left: Nader Daoud/AP Images; 21: csp_rosselladegradi/age fotostock; 22 left: travelpixs/Alamy Images; 22 right: Classic Image/Alamy Images; 23: mauritius images GmbH/Alamy Images; 25: Sean Pavone/Dreamstime; 26: Oriol Alamany/minden Pictures; 28: Val Duncan/Kenebec Images/Alamy Images; 29: Paolo Rossetti/Getty Images; 30: Michael Runkel/robertharding/Getty Images; 31: Herbert Kratky/ imageBROKER/age fotostock; 32: Kertu/Shutterstock; 34: Andre Seale/VWPics/Redux; 35: Dorit Bar-Zakay/ Getty Images; 36: Mattes René/age fotostock; 37 top: Ali Jarekji/Reuters; 37 bottom: Salah Malkawi/Getty Images; 38: Christian Kober/Robert Harding Picture Library; 40: Jake Lyell/Alamy Images; 42: Nick Brundle Photography/Getty Images; 43: Album/Alamy Images; 44: Hanan Isachar/Getty Images; 46: Military History Collection/Alamy Images; 49: AFP/Getty Images; 50: Charles Hewitt/Picture Post/Getty Images; 51: Frank Scherschel/The LIFE Picture Collection/Getty Images; 53: Martyn Hayhow/AFP/Getty Images; 54: Universal History Archive/UIG/Getty Images; 56: John MacDougall/Pool Photo/AP Images; 58: Salah Malkawi/Getty Images; 59: Barry Iverson/The LIFE Images Collection/Getty Images; 61 top: Raga Jose Fuste/age fotostock; 62: Salah Malkawi/ Getty Images; 63: Heba Kanso/Thomson Reuters Foundation; 64: Lindsey Leger/ZUMA Press, Inc./Alamy Images; 65: Muhammad Hamed/Reuters; 66: ZoranKrstic/Shutterstock; 67: Jordan Pix/Getty Images; 68: Steve Outram/Robert Harding Picture Library; 72: David Shwatal/Alamy Images; 73: Bill Lyons/ Alamy Images; 74: Bill Lyons/Alamy Images; 75: Alvaro Fuente/NurPhoto/Getty Images; 76: Joel Carillet/ Getty Images; 79: Jordan Pix/ Getty Images; 80: Tien Tran/newzulu/Alamy Images; 81: Didi/Alamy Images; 82: Khalil Mazraawi/AFP/Getty Images; 83: Thomas Imo/Photothek/Getty Images; 85: Lee Christensen/Getty Images; 86: robertharding/Alamy Images; 88: Zev rad/bibleland/Alamy Images; 89: Thomas Imo/Photothek/ Getty Images; 90: Sirio Carnevalino/Shutterstock; 91: Majed Jaber/Reuters; 92: Francoise De Mulder/Roger Viollet/Getty Images; 93: csp_vladj55/age fotostock; 94: Muhammad Hamed/Reuters; 95: Mohammad Abu Ghosh/Xinhua/Alamy Images; 96: Ton Koene/age fotostock; 97: Khalil Mazraawi/AFP/Getty Images; 98: Gareth Dewar/Alamy Images; 99: Jordan Pix/ Getty Images; 100: Yadid Levy/Alamy Images; 102: Jon Arnold/ age fotostock; 103: Ali Jarekji/Reuters; 104: Andreas Solaro/AFP/Getty Images; 105: Juliane Thiere/Alamy Images; 106: Sergi Reboredo/Alamy Images; 107: NJT90/Wikimedia; 108: Giles Keyte/ 20th Century Fox Film Corp. All rights reserved/Courtesy Everett Collection; 109: Graziano Arici/age fotostock; 110: Rafael Ben-Ari/Chamel/age fotostock; 111 top: Evan Vucci/AP Images; 111 bottom: Kevin Lamarque/Reuters; 113: Shinji Akagi/Far East Press/AFLO/Newscom; 114: Issei Kato/Reuters; 115: Awad Awad/AFP/Getty Images; 116: Lutz Jaekel/laif/Redux; 118: RooM the Agency/Alamy Images; 119: Yadid Levy/Alamy Images; 120: Majed Jaber/Reuters; 121: Mark Hannaford/Getty Images; 123: Yusuf Gunaydin/The Picture/Alamy Images; 124: bonchan/Shutterstock; 125: Riehle/laif/Redux; 127: Mohammad Abu Ghosh/Xinhua/Alamy Images; 130 left: ZoranKrstic/Shutterstock; 130 right: Maher Attar/Sygma/Getty Images; 131 right: csp_rosselladegradi/age fotostock; 133 center left: David Shwatal/Alamy Images; 133 bottom left: Didi/Alamy Images; 133 bottom right: Awad Awad/AFP/Getty Images.

Maps by Mapping Specialists.